Thanks Merv,
for your help in
making our Youth Conference
a success.

Youth Conference Committee
June 1987

THE *Sensitive* LEADER

THE *Sensitive* LEADER

Dennis L. Lythgoe

Deseret Book Company
Salt Lake City, Utah

To my dad

ISBN 0-87579-061-5

First printing November 1986

CONTENTS

PREFACE

As members of The Church of Jesus Christ of Latter-day Saints, we all find ourselves "in charge" in many different settings: in our homes, our neighborhoods, our communities, and the Church. Often we are catapulted into leadership responsibilities without adequate preparation. We may feel uneasy and find ourselves struggling for answers to difficult problems. We may ask advice from those around us, read whatever we can find, and pray. We make mistakes, suffer embarrassments, and finally begin to improve and to feel more comfortable making decisions and leading others. No matter how we approach it, the process is painful. This book is designed to ease the pain and to offer insights and suggestions on the varying aspects of successful leadership.

In gathering the material for this book, I have utilized my own experiences as a leader, the experiences of people I have known over the years, and those of successful leaders who have shared their knowledge with me. I realize that leadership can be a controversial subject. Not all of us see the same qualities in a successful leader, nor do we emulate the same leaders. Some of us are impressed with bureaucratic techniques that may be evident in the business world, while others are more appreciative of the spiritual qualities. I have always preferred the latter. It is my belief that those leaders who succeed are those who are most interested in nourishing and strengthening human relationships.

The preeminent example of leadership in my life came

to me from my father, Leo T. Lythgoe, who passed away in September 1985 just three days short of his ninetieth birthday. My brother and sisters and our families had gathered in Salt Lake City, Utah, a few days before his birthday, to plan a major celebration—which never took place. It seemed characteristic of him that he would assemble all of us in one place, visit with us appreciatively, and then leave *before* the celebration. He had always disliked fanfare and did not enjoy being fussed over.

Throughout his life Dad was an incredibly cheerful and optimistic man who would invariably wake me in the mornings singing "Oh it's nice to get up in the morning in the good old summer time. It's nice to get up in the morning, but it's nicer to stay in your bed!" Then he would start yanking on the covers. I used to wonder how anyone could be so unfailingly cheerful in the mornings, but now I find myself behaving in the same incorrigible manner with my own children. In many ways I can see the direct impact on my life of my father's personality and style. For years I have found myself uttering his exact phrases at the dinner table, while giving my young children baths, and in a host of other situations.

I have often thought that it was fortunate that my father's influence on me was positive, because it was certainly profound. He was a gentle man with deep feelings, a strong sentimental streak, and an easy tendency to tears. I often blamed him for my own inability to control my emotions. He was embarrassed about it, just as I am. In public he would make obvious, awkward efforts to mask his tears by clearing his throat and coughing. Everyone who knew him identified it immediately as one of his most endearing qualities.

When he was only twelve years old, Dad's mother died. His father's work often took him away from his family for days and sometimes months. As a young boy, Dad was in charge of the farm for five months while his father was gone on a timber haul. He remembered being scared when he went to bed alone in their little log house. "Land," he once told me, "it was darker than a stack of black cats in that town. There were *no* lights, you know. Pa wasn't home, and I'd go climb into bed scared to death. But I'd go to bed, and I'd soon be to sleep."

All my life my dad taught me to work, to be dependable, and to never quit one job until I had another. His own love of work was evident over the years as he gave everything he had, whether it was in the service, on a mission to California, or on the job for twenty-eight years at the D & RG Railroad. He worked for nineteen years for the County Water System, where he put in twelve hour days and was constantly on call. In spite of the hassles and emergencies, he said: "It kept me *interested!* It kept me *thinking.* I had to figure out how to regulate it. It kept me a jumping every bloomin' minute." Most of all, he devoted himself to his family.

This spiritual man was natural and unaffected. When I asked him if his patriarchal blessing had been correct when it said he would have dreams and see visions, he said, "Well, I had hunches all right, I guess." He was inspiring to us and always made family decisions under the guidance of the Spirit. Actually, he was the instrument through which I received my testimony of the gospel.

Dad was deeply in love with Mom for fifty-six years. Their courtship was unabashedly romantic. Dad took her rowing at Liberty Park, sang "Row, Row, Row," stopped and tried unsuccessfully (according to Mom) to kiss her, and then he sang their song, "Let Me Call You Sweetheart." When Dad bought Lizzie, a new 1928 Chevrolet, he'd take Mom for rides all over the valley—from Ogden to Provo. It was during one of those long rides that they got engaged.

They were happily married for fifty-four years and had the most completely devoted and loving relationship I have ever seen. In their last years together when Mom became ill, Dad filled her every need without any complaint. When she died in January 1984, he was devastated. He missed her desperately and continued to hear her voice calling him in the middle of the night. In the last six months of his life, he grew tired of his earthly limitations and longed for Mom.

Now that he has joined her, I am grateful for the consistent example he was for me. He was not a corporate giant. He was, rather, a dynamic, resolute leader of his family, and a warm, dependable example to his friends. To me, he symbolized leadership at its best.

This book, therefore, is dedicated to the premise that effective leadership is administered only through love, compassion, and respect for people and their feelings. It is based on the belief that all of us can learn to be better leaders through hard work, by practicing the principles of the Savior, by learning from other leaders, and by developing sensitivity to human needs.

There are paradoxes. Those who lead effectively should always be in the humble service of others; yet they need to have enough self-assurance to inspire the confidence of followers. Leaders should be teachers who can explain and instill concepts in people, as well as administrators who can organize and plan effectively. Leaders need to be enough removed from their followers to be accepted in their roles; yet they should be willing to mingle freely with their followers, to be sincerely interested in their problems and joys. More important than any of these, leaders should be sensitive to the Spirit, and retain and cultivate the ability to listen. I have tried to address these issues in a way that will enrich the lives and experiences of present or future leaders. I hope to provide answers to some of their problems and to give specific advice for dealing with many different situations. I believe that we can all apply principles of Christian living to enhance our effectiveness as leaders— wherever and whenever we're in charge.

Chapter One

LEADERSHIP BY EXAMPLE

Whether it be as church leaders, teachers, parents, or friends, we all have the opportunity to lead by example. Harold B. Lee once said, "How can I hear what you say when what you *do* rings so loudly in my ears?"[1] All of us are aware that when we use an unfortunate phrase at the dinner table, criticize a neighbor, or tell an unseemly story, our children are quick to follow in our footsteps. How much more preferable it is that the example we set for others be a positive one.

Matthew records that Jesus, while walking by the sea in Galilee, saw Peter and Andrew casting a net into the sea. "And he saith unto them, Follow me, and I will make you fishers of men. And they straightway left their nets, and followed him." (Matthew 4:18-20.) Nephi records Jesus' visit to the American continent and his vital question, "Therefore, what manner of men ought ye to be? Verily I say unto you, even as I am." (3 Nephi 27:27.)

The scriptures are rich with Jesus' references to the power of example and his expectations that those he taught would follow him. President Spencer W. Kimball said Christ's was a "program of 'do what I do,' rather than 'do what I say.' His innate brilliance would have permitted him to put on a dazzling display, but that would have left his followers behind. He walked and worked with those he was to serve. His was not a long-distance leadership. He was not afraid of close friendships; he was not afraid that proximity to him would disappoint his followers. The leaven of true leadership cannot lift others unless we are with and serve those to be led."[2]

The example of Jesus was one of humility. The successful leader in whatever field, in spiritual or secular pursuits, is unlikely to command respect by demonstrating love of power, status, or title. A leader who is obsessed with having the follower show deference to him has probably already been surpassed by the follower. I have known some church leaders who demanded that people recognize them verbally by their titles. I observed a mission president lose his sense of dignity when he demanded the recognition he felt had not been accorded him in a church conference session. Leaning self-consciously toward the pulpit, he whispered loudly in the ears of the person conducting, "Be sure to tell them I'm *here!*" In another case, a bishop who was fearful that his status was not being correctly acknowledged when a ward member addressed him by his first name, awkwardly ordered, "Call me *bishop!*" In both cases, the result was a loss of respect. By insisting that his title guaranteed respect, each leader betrayed his own sense of insecurity when he should have realized that being close to a follower in no way diminishes a leader.

Lowell L. Bennion said, "I have less interest in exaltation now than I used to have. I don't want to be exalted. I'd like to be in the presence of Christ, be a coworker, but I believe that he who would save his life shall lose it, and he that would lose his life shall find it."[3] The Master himself said, "For whosoever exalteth himself shall be abased; and he that humbleth himself shall be exalted." (Luke 14:11.)

Many years ago, I lived in a ward that experienced a rather startling change of leadership. The first bishop was an assertive, highly organized man who enjoyed talking at length in public about his own accomplishments in an effort to inspire us to similar feats. He was impressed with statistics and insisted on results that could be measured. He also thrived on being called "Bishop," and became irritated if anyone called him "Brother."

When this bishop was released, we could not imagine anyone stepping into his forceful, even charismatic shoes. The new bishop turned out to be opposite in almost every respect. He was seemingly unconcerned about statistics and instead concentrated on individual expressions of love and interest in the members. He seemed almost unaware of titles and persisted in introducing himself to new members by his first name. Yet, ironically, we *wanted* to call him "Bishop" because he seemed to clearly deserve the office. He seemed always willing to sacrifice his own time and pleasures to help a member in distress, and he did it in a gentle, approachable way. When I became aware that a neighbor of mine was a victim of emotional distress, I called the bishop and expressed my concerns. Within half an hour he was at my doorstep, and together we went to talk to my neighbor. It appeared to me that this bishop exemplified the admonition of the Savior when He said, "follow me." Although Jesus was capable of being assertive, he was described as a man of unusual compassion, and humility—the qualities we need to emulate most.

Young people need exemplary leaders to point their lives in the right direction. Wendell J. Ashton once advised young boys to "walk quietly, as in stocking feet, but fearlessly, in faith."[4] In the opinion of Walter MacPeek, "Boys need lots of heroes like Lincoln and Washington. But they also need to have some heroes close by. They need to know some man of towering strength and basic integrity, personally. They need to meet them on the street, to hike and camp with them, to see them in close-to-home, everyday, down-to-earth situations; to feel close enough to them to ask questions and to talk things over man-to-man with them."[5]

As a young boy growing up in the Church, I remember such relationships with bishops, members of bishoprics, and home teachers. I recall going to the stake farm for the graveyard irrigation shift with a man who was a counselor in the ward bishopric. Together we tromped around the dark furrows, minding the flow of the water during the night. Afterward, he became a bishop, then a stake president, a temple president, and finally a regional representative of the Quorum of the Twelve—and he never stopped being warm, personal, and approachable.

As a young deacon, my first home teaching companion was a distinguished, venerable man who set an admirable example of leadership for me. He was clearly dedicated to helping our assigned families, even if he had to speak candidly to them. Together we taught some young families who were semiactive in the Church. He did not hesitate to call them to repentance, a tendency that made me uncomfortable. But he had a gentle quality that they admired, and no one ever seemed angry with him. He made sure that I had my own opportunity to present lessons to these people, and he praised me vigorously afterward. When I gave talks in church, he was always the first to the stand to compliment me. Through love and example he seemed the epitome of leadership.

My next home teaching companion was my own father, unquestionably the most gentle man I have ever known. I never remember him calling anyone to repentance, but he was continually rushing to help someone in need. The families we visited seemed assured that he was willing to assist them in a variety of different ways. Dad was also impressed with my lesson presentation style, and was perfectly content to conduct meetings while I gave the message. He enjoyed remaining in the background, never needing the adulation of the world to give him self-confidence. In his quiet, resolute way he taught me more than other leaders or teachers.

As President Kimball said, "None of us should become so busy in our formal Church assignments that there is no room left for quiet Christian service to our neighbors."[6] Unfortunately, our lives can become so easily filled that there seems no way to fit in Christian service. As members of a lay church, Mormons sometimes accept numerous assignments and callings, and then assume that their duty is done. In fact, their lives may already be too crowded to pay proper attention to their own families. When that happens, it is time to step back and reassess priorities. The Lord gave us this injunction. "Men should be anxiously engaged in a good cause, and do many things of their own free will, and bring to pass much righteousness," which may be the ultimate test of living the gospel. (D&C 58:27.) Being a leader in the Church should never be considered license to neglect the "weightier matters of the law."

A woman named Helen was called to be a Relief Society president rather late in life. She was shocked at the call but approached it with enthusiasm and courage. She was blessed with an abundance of life's experiences, both happy and sad, and she was able to use them effectively in visiting and counseling the women of her ward. Almost immediately the women loved her, for her wisdom, her gentle manner, and her unmistakable interest in them. Although she was affluent, no one ever thought of her as elite. She never considered herself above anyone, and she invited women into her home on a social basis. She visited with them in small groups, and she initiated one-on-one meetings that gave her the opportunity to know each person and for each person to get to know her. She always seemed to have energy to expend for something unstructured or unscheduled.

Another woman, Diane, served for several years as a ward and stake public communications director. She loved the work and treated it almost as a full-time job. She remained energetic and anxious about the need to acquaint people with the Church and its people, and she worked tirelessly to submit articles and photographs to local newspapers. Even in the face of rejection, she remained optimistic. People who worked under her thought her personality was infectious, and she was universally regarded as the most effective missionary in her ward. In spite of these successes, she had problems and disappointments of her own, especially in her home life. Her husband never joined the Church, and one of her sons was so seriously injured that his life hung in the balance for months. While troubled, she continued to serve and inspire others.

One calling that is especially persuasive in its potential influence on young people is that of Young Women's president. I have known several outstanding women who excelled in that call. Marilyn exuded warmth, personality, and genuine interest in the young women of her ward. She was so charismatic to them that they felt literally drawn into her circle of interest. She drove great distances to transport young women to important events, and she never seemed to lose an opportunity to contribute something unique to each young woman's life. The young women obviously loved her and considered her a trusted confidante and role model.

Marti, my own wife, exemplified the same unusual commitment and example as a stake Young Women's president. For years she devoted her time and her creativity to the young women of our stake. At our stake girls' camp, many people were impressed with her spirit and enthusiasm, and they said that it inspired them. When I asked her about it, she was amazed. "I was exhausted," she said. "How could I have inspired them?" A stake calling often brings more relationships with other leaders than it does with the rank and file, but Marti generated warm friendships with young women across the stake who continue to hold her in great admiration. She worked very hard at it, and always initiated projects that blessed the lives of many young women.

Ardeth Kapp, general president of the Young Women asked: "Can the local leaders reach the youth . . . these youth of a noble birthright . . . these leaders who, in most cases, are but youth themselves in gospel experiences? Yes, they can and they will. I see the influence of the Young Women of this Church, the local units moving as a mighty force across the face of the entire earth, rising up in defense of the truth."[7]

In an *Ensign* magazine article, Sister Kapp related the story of Joan of Arc, born in 1412 in France, a woman who had a mission to fulfill. Sister Kapp said: "Her whole soul seemed to yearn toward God and country. This young girl became the heroine of France. Joan of Arc at the age of nineteen was burned at the stake. From the play 'Joan of Lorraine,' by Maxwell Anderson, her words serve as a reminder of a young woman committed to her values: 'I know this too now: Every man gives his life for what he believes. Every woman gives her life for what she believes. Sometimes people believe in little or nothing, nevertheless they give up their lives to that little or nothing. One life is all we have, and we live it as we believe in living it, and then it's gone. But to surrender what you are, and live without belief—that's more terrible than dying—more terrible than dying young.'"

According to Sister Kapp, Joan of Arc was committed at a tender age to stand up and lead out. "The Lord asks that you let your light shine, not a borrowed light, not merely a reflected light, but the light within you generated from obedience to the gospel of Jesus Christ, from eternal values, uncompromised values. These values make possible a constant awareness of who you are and what it means to be a young woman in The Church of Jesus Christ of Latter-day Saints.

"These are your challenges and promises. These are your days in the history of the kingdom. Together we can make of them days never to be forgotten. Together we can pledge to listen for the call and then answer, 'I will. Send me to stand up and lead out.'"[8]

Yet balance is so important. S. Dilworth Young once said, "Each of has the same general calling. The Lord will not hold us blameless if we allow organizational responsibility, or the lack of it, to interfere with the duty to care for those around us."[9] A leader who endeavors to do many things of his or her own free will commands infinitely greater respect than one who browbeats his followers about doing their duty.

When I was a college student, Lowell L. Bennion was the director of the LDS Institute of Religion adjacent to the University of Utah. I was able to observe in numerous instances his efforts on behalf of both students and other people who needed him. For instance, at Christmastime he regularly handpicked a group of carolers to travel around the Salt Lake Valley and sing to people he knew who were shut-ins. It took considerable effort to organize this project, involving hours of practice as well as travel on the selected day, but he loved doing it. Those of us who participated were personally enriched, but we could also see that Lowell Bennion did not have to do it. He did it because he believed in it and in the people we visited. His continued interest in the poor and disadvantaged, resulting in specific acts of kindness and courage, taught us admiration for him that words or organizational prowess may never have accomplished.

I have some friends who represent an excellent example of loving, voluntary service. After their children grew up, married, and had their own families, this couple decided to take foster children into their home. They were drawn to children who were disadvantaged in various ways and needed special care. Over the years they have had many children with a variety of emotional and physical problems. Most recently, they have two young children who need such extensive care that the couple is often left in an exhausted state, yet they continue their efforts. They love the feeling of fulfillment it brings and whatever small improvements they see in the children. When I asked the woman why she took these children in, she said it was because her own parents had adopted her, and they loved her in a completely devoted way, setting a supreme example of love and leadership. She said she was just doing the same things she had seen her adoptive parents do for her.

People usually follow only those leaders who exemplify what they say. When I was a missionary in New Zealand, we often repeated the saying, "As the supervising elder goes [district leader today] so goes the district." Elder J. Thomas Fyans commented: "Do you see what is being suggested? It is called church government by example. You know as I know that a stake presidency or bishopric will never inspire their stake or ward members to do something they are too busy to do themselves. I am impressed by the example offered by President Ezra Taft Benson who completed his family histories and four generation program before he addressed the Church on this subject in October 1978. Church government by example!"[10]

When I was called as a bishop, I was determined to inaugurate a system of visiting the membership of the ward on a regular basis so I could get to know each member personally. To make that goal more realistic, I decided to remove myself from the home teaching list. After all, I would be home teaching much more actively than other home teachers in the ward, and I would not be interpreted as showing favoritism toward those who had been assigned as my home teaching families. When I announced this intention to other ward leaders, there were discernible gasps and long faces. Without any explanation I could immediately tell that I had made a serious mistake. No matter how much time I may have spent visiting people in their homes, people would not think that I was setting an example as a home teacher if I did not have a regular home teaching route. It took only a few minutes for me to change my mind and retain my status as a home teacher.

The same principle is evident in the leadership we offer in the home. Speaking to the Nephites, Jacob said, "Wherefore, ye shall remember your children, how that ye have grieved their hearts because of the example that ye have set before them; and also, remember that ye may, because of your filthiness, bring your children unto destruction, and their sins be heaped upon your heads at the last day." (Jacob 3:10.) Unfortunately, few of us realize the kind of impression we are making on our children with every visible action. We believe we do not need to impress our own families. We hope they will love us and understand us in spite of our fatigue, our impatience, our lack of sensitivity or willingness to help in a crisis. This may be the biggest mistake that we can ever make in leadership. The truth is that our spouses and our children need to see the best side of us. We need to expend even more effort to serve them than we do to gain approval from the world. It is possible to be comfortable and relaxed at the end of a day without becoming completely self-indulgent.

In the early days of my marriage, I remember feeling the need to unwind when I came home. I taught classes professionally and in church, and so on Monday evenings I felt that it would be acceptable for me to prepare the family home evening lesson with noticeably less effort. I tended to rely on my wits and to improvise. Of course our children realized it immediately and gave less attention and respect to my message. It suddenly occurred to me that I was giving the *least* time to the instruction and development of the *most* important people in my life. It was also evident that teaching children of different ages was a more important challenge than teaching a controlled age group or a group with much in common. To be effective at home I needed more examples, more variety in subject matter, more visual aids, and I needed to be sensitive to the individual responses of each child.

Feeling "at home" is vital to our mental and psychological health, and all of us need that release; but we should think of being at home as a shift in gears or a change from the patterns of our day rather than a time to "check out." If we remain involved, we can be effective in listening and responding to the needs of our families in the manner they deserve. Alma had sage advice: "Suffer not yourself to be led away by any vain or foolish thing; suffer not the devil to lead away your heart . . . ; for when they saw your conduct they would not believe in my words." (Alma 39:11.) If we behave at our best in our jobs and in our church positions, and then come home and show our children a different side, the example may be devastating. Our challenge is to be consistent, loving examples of gospel principles.

The same level of comfort may sometimes develop in friendships or working relationships. A person who has worked with another for several months or years may feel comfortable enough to express candid opinions and to care little if a less sensitive self is on view. I am not advocating that we try to be people we are not, only that we realize that even those we know well deserve our best selves. Hugh B. Brown once said, "He who knows the precepts and neglects to obey them is like one that lights a candle in the darkness and then closes his eyes."[11]

It is vital not only that we be aware of the impression we make on others, but that we consciously cultivate a leadership style that will be effective. Leadership is rarely carried out successfully through subtle means alone. We cannot afford to hope that someone has the right idea, or assume that our wishes are understood. We need to formulate and express a strong example that others can follow. We need to endeavor to live a life that others will not find disappointing or shocking—or inconsistent with our reputations.

In an especially effective sermon, Elder Angel Abrea expressed this thought:

"A few years ago I found myself in a small city park that was covered with trees and adorned with monuments, a plaza typical of many found throughout Argentina. I was watching a sculptor as he used a hammer and chisel to put the finishing touches on his project. His artwork portrayed a mother holding a child in her arms.

"The artist was working to perfect the hands of the mother, which were fashioned of marble, and the results appeared to me to be masterful strokes in the sculptor's own style.

"As I stood there fascinated, eager to grasp knowledge of the artist's skills, a shoeshine boy passing by stopped and stood by me. After attentively watching the progress of the final touches for a few moments, the industrious young boy turned to me and in amazement asked, 'Sir, tell me, why is he breaking it now?'

"The youth's naive and unexpected query gave me cause to contemplate the examples that we constantly set, the impressions we give by our actions and our behavior. It made me realize how extremely important our examples can be, as is the force or weakness with which we convey our personal convictions in our every day life."[12]

The words of Paul came to Angel Abrea's mind: "For if the trumpet give an uncertain sound, who shall prepare himself to the battle?" (1 Corinthians 14:8.)

Barbara Winder, general Relief Society president of the Church, said: "We are sanctifying ourselves one step at a time as we accept personal responsibility for our actions and honor the covenants we make at baptism, in the temple, and as we take the sacrament each Sunday. We progress by living worthy to receive the blessings available to us, responding to those promptings to serve others, by loving one another, and by trying to obey the prophet's voice in all things. . . .

"From a Thai refugee camp, Mary Ellen Edmunds expressed it well for all of us when she said, 'For me I feel close to the Savior when I can do in a small way for someone else what He would do if He were there. In a way that's what being an instrument is all about, . . . to make it possible for his love to reach more of his children.'"[13]

Elder Marion D. Hanks told the story of a conversation between a Sunday School teacher and a little girl. The teacher asked the girl, "What does it mean to practice what you preach?" The young girl replied, "Oh, that means writing your talk and saying it over and over again before you give it in church."[14]

Similarly, we should live those principles in which we believe "over and over again," exhibiting to all we meet that we mean what we say. We should sanctify ourselves one step at a time by loving and serving one another. If we do not practice what we preach, we can never expect any discerning person to follow us. Leadership must radiate through example first.

Chapter Two

A LIFETIME OF SERVICE

Elaine Cannon, former general president of the Young Women, once said, "Service is not a project to be abandoned at the end of a Saturday afternoon—it's a lifetime investment in humanity."[1] Every leader should be primarily interested in service to others, whether it be in the family or in the Church. Since human relationships represent the most important aspects of everyday living, they need to be nurtured and cultivated.

One bishop announced to his counselors that they would each take turns sitting in the congregation with their families during sacrament meeting. There would be two of them remaining on the stand, enough to handle problems of presiding, and the third member of the bishopric could sit with his wife and help take care of his children. It seemed such an excellent example to have the bishopric sit in the congregation with no loss of status, and show the ward members that they felt responsible for their families.

The counselors loved the idea, and the bishop decided to implement it immediately. The following Sunday they began the new policy, which caused a genuine stir throughout the congregation. Many people responded with enthusiasm, saying that it caused them to feel a new rapport with their leaders. Others thought it impressive that the children in the ward could see the members of the bishopric devote equal time to the care of their own families. But there were criticisms, too, especially from the new members of the ward. They thought the process was dis-

14

quieting, a sign that the bishopric was not functioning fully, that they were abdicating their authority over the ward.

The experiment lasted only a few weeks. It soon became apparent that the stake president was not enthusiastic about it. He told the bishop that he might approve of the counselors alternating turns with their families in the congregation, but he believed that the members should always be able to look at the stand and see their bishop. He thought they needed that dependable anchor.

Though this experiment was short-lived, the motivation behind it should not be. Jesus said, "Whosoever will be great among you, shall be your minister." (Mark 10:43-44.) Another version was "Whosoever will be chief among you, let him be your servant." (Matthew 20:27.)

One of the more impressive scriptural examples of one willing to serve is King Benjamin, who tried to serve his people with all his might, mind, and strength. He said: "And even I, myself, have labored with mine own hands that I might serve you, and that ye should not be laden with taxes, and that there should nothing come upon you which was grievous to be borne—and of all things which I have spoken, ye yourselves are witnesses this day." (Mosiah 2:14.)

He wanted his people to understand that he had no desire to boast of such service, that he had only been in the service of his God. "And behold, I tell you these things that ye may learn wisdom; that ye may learn that when ye are in the service of your fellow beings ye are only in the service of your God."(Mosiah 2:17.)

He also told his people that he expected them to render the same form of service to those around them. "And also, ye yourselves will succor those that stand in need of your succor; ye will administer of your substance unto him that standeth in need; and ye will not suffer that the beggar putteth up his petition to you in vain, and turn him out to perish." (Mosiah 4:16.)

T. Edgar Lyon, a noted historian and teacher, once gave me some advice that his father had given him based on his many years of service as a bishop. "Love your people!" As I became steadily more immersed in detail over the next several years, I tried to retain that simple but profound thought. James R. Moss advised leaders everywhere to love all of the sheep. "Remember in the parable of the lost sheep that when it was found, the shepherd 'rejoiceth more of that sheep, than of the ninety and nine which went not astray.' (Matthew 18:13.) Successful leaders love *all* of their followers, not just those who follow the best."[2]

It is easy for a leader to exempt himself from service to those who may seem less worthy or unacceptable for reasons relating to personality, interests, politics, or some other reason. I knew a church leader who categorized people as desirable or undesirable to associate with on the basis of their political beliefs. He failed to recognize that political philosophy had no place in the loving relationships so necessary in church work. It is even more important under such circumstances that service be rendered and that love be expressed.

A Relief Society president was troubled that two women found it difficult to support her for personal reasons. They avoided her socially and never relied on her help in times of trouble. She worried about both women and tried in small ways to reach them, expressing interest and love through anonymous service.

Then one day during a regular interview, the stake Relief Society president issued a challenge to her. She asked her to concentrate special effort on anyone in the ward she might have offended. The stake Relief Society president suggested that such people needed her help even more than other women in the ward, and asked that she fast, pray, and make diligent efforts to improve the relationship. It was an insightful challenge, and she accepted it. Over the next several weeks she made greater efforts to communicate with those people and to befriend them. In one case it seemed that there was no success. This person continued to snub her and to speak ill of her; but the other woman was touched. There was measurable, impressive progress. Over time this woman became her genuine friend, and subsequently requested that she participate in important family activities. Fifty percent success was valuable and heartening, and she managed to retain a healthy friendship that otherwise would have eluded her.

Camilla Kimball served as a visiting teacher in the Church for approximately sixty years. Her teaching usually took place on the first Tuesday of each month. She did not go to fulfill an assignment but to make friends. She said: "I think visiting teaching is the most important work we do in the Church. I feel I really know a woman only when I enter her home. In this way I can serve her person-to-person. I have tried not to suppress any inclination to generous word or deed."[3]

Barbara Smith, general president of the Relief Society for many years, expressed her belief in compassionate service, in visiting the fatherless or those in prison, caring for the needy, giving comfort to those who mourn, feeding the hungry, listening to the troubled heart, and giving water to those who thirst. Sister Smith recalled visiting with a woman who had been in an automobile accident that left her paralyzed from the neck down. Sister Smith said: "When I asked her how she was, she said, 'Spiritually I'm just fine. I have a good place to live, good care, wonderful visiting teachers I couldn't do without, and I know that the Lord lives and loves me.'"[4]

Laurel Ulrich, noted Mormon writer and teacher, has recalled vividly her experiences being a visiting teacher in inner-city Boston. She said: "I don't know whether the Relief Society president planned it that way, but tracking down obscure apartment buildings on one-way streets in dark corners of the city was as good a way as any to initiate a bright-faced young student wife from the West into the realities of urban life." Sister Ulrich remembered with sentimentality her regular visits to Sister Chan, who was relatively inactive in the Church and spoke little English. Sister Chan considered the visiting teachers to be "the Church" and always insisted on feeding them during their visits. They had many excellent Chinese meals as well as friendly conversation about the gospel. When Sister Ulrich left Boston, she paid a last visit to Sister Chan, who called her into a room of the apartment, pressed two bills into her hand, and said, "This is lucky money."

Laurel Ulrich felt dismay, thinking she had no right to accept money from someone who needed it more than she did. When she discovered that it was two ten-dollar bills, she worried about it so much that she mailed eighteen dollars to Sister Chan with a note. In it, she explained her suspicion that Sister Chan had intended to give her two dollars instead of twenty. She reasoned that Sister Chan's inadequate English could have been responsible for her mistaking the denomination of the bills.

"I am still ashamed of my stupidity," she confessed. Several months later, a friend wrote to me from Boston to say the Chans were offended by my letter, as of course they should have been.

"'What is twenty dollars,' they had said, 'when you might never see someone again?'

"I hope if Sister Chan still remembers me she has forgiven my insensitivity and my pride. I had tried to live by the visiting teachers' motto—it is more blessed to give than to receive. Looking back, I am astonished at how much I received and how little I was capable of giving."[5]

Such an experience illustrates effectively the depth of relationships that are possible with effective visiting teaching. Linda, a member of my ward, was a visiting teacher for many months to an inactive sister who felt so drawn to her visiting teacher that she thoroughly confided in her. Her marriage was unhappy, and she was contemplating divorce when she met Linda. As this miserable sister struggled with her problems, Linda encouraged her and counseled her. In the end, the sister sought a divorce, reevaluated her religious beliefs, and returned to the Church, becoming a dynamic and active member. Linda became her most important and trusted friend. In this case, visiting teaching represented an invaluable service that resulted in a changed and happier life for this sister and her children.

There are other much less structured ways that we can render significant service. In the Church we often have occasion to assist someone to move in or out of the ward. When people help others move, there are opportunities for friendship, lighthearted banter, and introspective conversation that are rare. In my experience, many people became friends in greater depth and loyalty at the end of a move. Many of them remembered the experience fondly for months or even years afterward.

I recall too well our own move to Massachusetts from Utah. We had enlisted the help of a professional mover whose van was supposed to predate our own arrival. Predictably, there were problems that resulted in a week's delay, with most of our possessions stranded in a New York warehouse. In the meantime, we had rented a duplex with no furniture. Our neighbors, a young couple with two children, rose to the occasion and brought us everything we needed: sleeping bags, kitchen utensils, TV trays to eat on, and so forth. Since then, these people have moved into a large home to accommodate their material prosperity. The husband has a thriving law practice that makes him one of the most prominent trial lawyers in the state. Nevertheless, he has never forgotten his commitment to service. Recently I called on him to lecture about his profession to a church group. Even though he is not a Latter-day Saint, he willingly accepted the invitation and presented a stimulating, invaluable look at his work, which most people regarded as the highlight of our conference. Although a prominent leader in his field, this man has retained a clear vision of the need for sacrifice and service. I will continue to fondly remember the TV trays and the sleeping bags.

Simple acts of service are well worth the sacrifice. My father seemed always willing to engage in such acts for his children. After a long, vigorous work day, he would drive any of us to various destinations, wait for us, bring us back, or come back later and pick us up. To a teenager who cannot yet drive, this was an important act of service, although I doubt that any of us were effusive in our praise of his actions. We knew it was his nature to give of himself; it was one of the reasons that we loved him.

The fact that my brother and sisters and I are all "in the driver's seat" now with our own children has allowed us to appreciate his unselfishness even more. Dad was also unfailingly patient in spending time with us and in trying to teach us. I noticed early in life that my dad was always available to neighbors, friends, and ward members, who would call him and request his help in finishing a home repair, moving a piece of furniture, digging out a septic tank, or taking an irrigation turn. He would willingly accept such invitations, often taking one of us along so that we could help him and learn about service. Sometimes he "asked" for these opportunities by wandering over to the neighbors when he got home from work to exchange some words about the day and inquire after their well being. They would frequently find something for him to do for them.

In our home, Marti is the exemplar of reliable and compassionate service to our children. On some days, she finds herself engaged in such tedious tasks as taking one of them to a department store to secure a new watchband, taking several of them ice skating because the teachers went to a convention, sewing up holes in clothes or hemming up pants, putting paper covers on school textbooks (a New England tradition), helping with homework even though it seems interminable, and reading to little Spencer. She always does it enthusiastically and somehow manages to keep up with her editing work, as well as her domestic re-

sponsibilities. The children obviously love her for it. It
shows especially when she is gone from home on church
assignments. They miss her and look forward to her return;
when she does, they are excited and anxiously share their
activities with her.

Even if children do not outwardly appreciate the level
of service offered by a parent, they will sometimes react by
offering acts of service themselves. When our twelve-year-
old son, David, brought home a catalog of products that his
school had asked him to sell for fund raising purposes, sixteen-year-old Kelly offered to take the catalog to her job
and try to interest some of her coworkers in it. She was successful, and David was very grateful.

When David's school schedule changed so that he
could not deliver his papers early enough to get to school
on time, Charlie inherited the paper route. Now when
Charlie needs help with the route or with collecting from
customers, David understands the need more clearly and is
more willing to serve than he used to be. As my new home
teaching companion, David is finding satisfaction in serving our families as we inquire about their needs and split
up the lesson. He is a people-oriented person, who enjoys
getting to know these people on a more intimate basis.

All of our children get an opportunity for service
through assigned acts of domestic responsibility: emptying
the dishwasher, setting the table, cleaning their rooms,
mowing the lawn. One of the dividends of such service is
the spawning of spontaneous acts of service that are done
freely, without compulsion.

In spite of scriptural advice that we be anxiously engaged in a good cause, it is common to assume that certain
people, because of their leadership roles and heavy com-
mitments to church work, should be exempted from participation in service or work projects. Clearly, the Lord
thought that there should be no status where service is concerned.

Hugh B. Brown said, "Too many men accept religion,

profess to love it, and cleave unto it, not from many unselfish motives but solely because of an inward peace, a
quieted conscience, and the radiant hope which they,
themselves, get from it. Religion then becomes not a
stimulus but a sedative. It is used not as an inspiration to
service, but as a substitute for service."[6]

Even while involved in leadership roles we may have
the opportunity to render acts of service that take us by surprise. A couple I know experienced a typical family crisis
when one of their youngest children became ill on a Sunday morning. Although she was the Gospel Doctrine
teacher and he was the bishop, they realized that one of
them would have to stay home with the child. After discussion, they settled on a compromise arrangement: he would
attend his early morning leadership meetings but return
home in time for her to travel to church to teach her class. It
seemed to them a clear case of family needs coming before
church leadership, and yet their compromise allowed each
of them to carry out some of their church responsibilities as
well.

Lowell Bennion has eloquently expressed concerns
about the possibility that church activity may interfere with
service: "We have a very elaborate program, so the faithful
Latter-day Saint is pretty well preoccupied with church life,
church activity and tends to identify the religious life with
church life. But that doesn't leave much time or motivation
to go beyond the boundaries of the church program into
the larger community. That concerns me.

"I'm also fearful that we emphasize the unique things
of Mormonism, rather than the basic core which is disci-
pleship of Christ. We ought to go to church to be motivated
and moved to go out and love our neighbor and do things
in a practical way, both within the Church and outside it in
the larger community. We should practice Christianity, not
just 'Churchianity.' Some do, of course, but I think there's
a tendency to concentrate on unique doctrines like the
Word of Wisdom, instead of those teachings which move

us really to carry out the eighteenth chapter of Mosiah: 'Bear one another's burdens, comfort those who stand in need of comfort,' and establish a *real* Christian community."[7]

President Kimball noted that "organizational lines in the Church have become walls that have kept us from reaching out to individuals as completely as we should. We will also find as we become less concerned with getting organizational or individual credit that we will become more concerned with serving the one whom we are charged to reach. We will also find ourselves becoming less concerned with our organizational identity and more concerned with our true and ultimate identity as a son or daughter of our Father in Heaven and helping others to achieve the same sense of belonging."

According to President Kimball, it is wise for all leaders to reflect on the qualities of their own past leaders, asking which had been most influential and why. "On reflecting for a few moments, you are apt to conclude that such a person really cared for you, that he or she took time for you, or that he or she taught you something you needed to know. Reflect now upon your performance, as I do on my own, as to whether or not we now embody in our own ministry those same basic attributes. It is less likely in stirring through one's memories that someone will be remembered because that individual was particularly influential because of a technique. Most often someone has served and helped us by giving us love and understanding, by taking time to assist us, and by showing us the way through the light of their own example. I cannot stress enough, therefore, the importance of our doing these same things for those who now depend upon us, just as we have depended upon others to serve us in the past by special leadership and special teaching."[8]

I have been impressed by simple acts of service that had no connection with the Church, but which seemed vital for understanding leadership at any level. Once, when struggling to start an ailing car, I took a gas can and rode a bike to a nearby service station. On the way home, the can of gasoline became unwieldy, causing me to walk with the can and the bike. My awkward appearance on a rainy day caught the eye of my mailman, who stopped and offered to put me and my bike in the back of his van. With breathless gratitude I accepted his offer.

Not too many weeks later, I found my mailman stuck in front of my neighbor's house on a snowy day, his wheels spinning hopelessly. I was able to return his favor by giving him the necessary push to get out. After that, he came to my door to tell me that he was interested in moving to Colorado, hoping for better economic circumstances. He had noticed that many Western publications, emanating from Utah and other Western states, were addressed to me. He wondered if I could give him information about Colorado and the West. Once he had acquired some material to read, he studied about Colorado before taking a flight to Denver to consider the possibility of transferring to the post office of a small Colorado town. I was heartened that I had been able to play a helpful role to this man that I barely knew. Small acts of service can have a contagious quality.

President Kimball said: "So often, our acts of service consist of simple encouragement or of giving mundane help with mundane tasks, but what glorious consequences can flow from mundane acts and from small but deliberate deeds!"[9] Those who have read Edward and Andrew Kimball's best-selling biography of President Kimball will remember the story of his assistance to a young mother in the Chicago airport. She had a two-year-old daughter and was stranded by bad weather without money, food, or clean clothing for the child. Under doctor's instructions, she was not supposed to carry the child unless absolutely necessary. Waiting in line, she kept pushing the crying child along the floor with her foot. Without being introduced, President Kimball noticed this woman and offered to help.

The mother later reported: "He lifted my sobbing little daughter from the cold floor and lovingly held her to him while he patted her gently on the back. He asked if she could chew a piece of gum. When she was settled down, he carried her with him and said something kindly to the others in the line ahead of me, about how I needed their help. They seemed to agree and then he went up to the ticket counter . . . and made arrangements with the clerk for me to be put on a flight leaving shortly. He walked with us to a bench, where we chatted a moment, until he was assured that I would be fine. He went on his way. About a week later I saw a picture of Apostle Spencer W. Kimball and recognized him as the stranger in the airport."[10]

President Gordon B. Hinckley once said that President Kimball "has embraced the whole membership in that spirit of brotherhood and mutual concern, which are the very heart of the gospel of the Master."

I once came to know personally of President Kimball's love for others. Several years ago, my mother developed a sore on her lip, which failed to heal. The family worried about it and urged her to seek medical attention, but she refused. She wanted to treat it in her own way, and she had doubts about the efficacy of medical science. Her own treatment did not work, and the sore grew larger. Members of the family urged her to see a physician, and we had help from local Church leaders, but she still refused. Finally, I contacted a General Authority for whom I had special respect and asked for his help. He responded kindly and invited me to bring her to his office, where he told her the story of his own skin cancer and its removal by a physician. He urged my mother to take the same course. The visit seem inspired. Before we left, he gave her a beautiful blessing in which he promised her that if she would seek medical help that she would "live long and bless many." Although she was very impressed with the experience, she still resisted medical treatment.

Three years later, in 1976, I reached a point of incredible

frustration. The sore had grown so large that she was embarrassed to go out and had great difficulty eating. Many
people grew impatient with her. We took comfort from
King Benjamin's admonition in the Book of Mormon to administer to those in need. "Perhaps thou shalt say: The
man has brought upon himself his misery; therefore I will
stay my hand, . . . for his punishments are just—but I say
unto you, O man, whosoever doeth this the same hath
great cause to repent; and except he repenteth of that
which he hath done he perisheth forever, and hath no interest in the Kingdom of God." (Mosiah 4:17-18.)

In desperation, I wrote a letter to President Kimball, recounted the history of my mother's sore and our difficulty
persuading her to go to a physician, and asked him if there
was any way he could help. Soon afterward, his secretary
called my mother and endeavored to make an appointment
for her to see the president in his office. Although she
wanted very much to see him, she was in a weakened condition, had suffered a fainting spell, and was so distressed
that she hesitated to go. The next day, President Kimball
called and conversed with her on the phone for approximately half an hour. He told her of his own medical history, suggested that his own life had been saved through
medical science, and implored her to see a physician and
have the sore treated. He was gentle, yet firm, and he did it
with a touch of humor. He told her that he and the other
brethren would pray for her at their regular temple meeting. Immediately afterward, my mother agreed to seek
medical help. She entered a hospital and with the help of a
renowned cancer specialist, the cancer was arrested
through radiation treatments. As a result of the direct interest and intervention of the prophet, her life was prolonged
for another eight years before she finally passed away in
her late seventies.

Again, President Kimball said: "God does notice us,
and he watches over us. But it is usually through another
person that he meets our needs. Therefore, it is vital that

we serve each other in the kingdom. The people of the Church need each other's strength, support, and leadership in a community of believers as an enclave of disciples."[11] The Lord has encouraged us to "succor the weak, lift up the hands which hang down, and strengthen the feeble knees." (D&C 81:5.)

Shortly after my mother's death, I was visiting in my father's High Priests group. The group leader asked me what my father, in his old age and grief, needed. My immediate reaction was to say that food brought periodically into the house would be helpful. By the time I visited Dad again, several months later, I realized that I should have said something else: as helpful as food is, what my father really needed were visits from caring people who would engage him in conversation and express sincere interest and love for him.

After reaching that realization, I had a sudden inspiration to take Dad to visit a former missionary companion of his who lived in Provo, Utah. Besides their missionary experiences together, they had much in common. They had both lost their wives, they were about the same age, and they loved and respected each other. Heber Winterton was very glad to greet my dad that day. The two of them thoroughly enjoyed the next two hours reminiscing, remembering people and events, laughing and crying about specific incidents. Their memories were remarkably keen, and they literally sparkled as they conversed. Heber revealed, among other things, that he had been responsible for transferring Dad from Nevada to California during the last months of his mission. He also told Dad for the first time the very moving story of how he had acquired his own testimony of the gospel while serving as a new missionary.

I was impressed by the importance of this occasion— the meeting of two old friends who had not seen each other for a good talk in many years—and the way their spirits were regenerated by each other. It was a small, simple thing to bring them together, but it made me think that we all need to be more creative in finding those acts of service that are genuinely productive.

Mother Teresa, the Yugoslavian nun who won the Nobel Peace Prize for her work among the very poor of India, experienced the healing and strengthening power of love in the lives of people with severe problems. Her prime dedication is to help people by sharing the love of God with them. In describing her philosophy of service, she said: "Be kind and merciful. Let no one ever come to you without coming away better and happier. Be the living expression of God's kindness: kindness in your face, kindness in your eyes, kindness in your smile, kindness in your warm greeting. In the slums we are the light of God's kindness to the poor. To children, to the poor, to all who suffer and are lonely, give always a happy smile. Give them not only your care, but also your heart."[12]

Perhaps this question from Micah expresses it best: "What doth the LORD require of thee, but to do justly, and to love mercy, and to walk humbly with thy God?" (Micah 6:8.) Every person who would be a leader should make this precept the preeminent one in his or her life.

Chapter Three

CONFIDENCE VERSUS HUMILITY

It is comforting to know that our leaders are human and therefore fallible. A story is told of Elder Heber C. Kimball, who sought hospitality from various people during his missionary travels, and a widow who fed him bread and milk and provided a room for him to spend the night. When he went into the bedroom to retire, she decided it was her opportunity to hear what an apostle sounded like when he prayed to the Lord. After the door was closed, she quietly crept to it and listened. First she heard Elder Kimball sitting on the bed, then each of his shoes falling loudly to the floor. Finally she heard him lean back on the bed and utter these words: "Oh Lord, bless Heber, he is so tired," and that was all. Later in life, Elder Kimball, as a member of the First Presidency, was leading his large family in prayer. In the middle of the prayer, he stopped speaking suddenly and broke out laughing. After he collected himself, he said, "Excuse me Lord, but it makes me laugh to think of some of the people I have to pray for," and then he finished his prayer.

Bruce R. McConkie used these examples to support the theme that the General Authorities are human. He said: "They told me they would like to record this, and I said that was all right, provided nobody ever heard it at 47 East South Temple, [Church Headquarters] because I enjoyed my membership in the Church."[1] Actually, most of us are relieved to hear such examples; we like to look up to leaders, but we also are gratified when we learn that they are not perfect. Much of American folklore is based on stories that depict leaders in all aspects of society as down-to-earth and believable human beings. Much folklore in Mormonism concerns J. Golden Kimball, a General Authority and a descendant of Heber C. Kimball, but some of it has centered on Spencer W. Kimball as well. For instance, the most famous anecdote about President Kimball may be the one about a man who stepped into an elevator in the LDS Church Office Building, noticed Spencer Kinard, who delivers the "Spoken Word" during Tabernacle Choir broadcasts, and said casually, "Push three for me, will you, Spence?" Spencer Kimball, who was also on the elevator, replied, "Surely," and pushed the button. The man was mortified at having appeared to have called the president of the Church "Spence," but President Kimball was not offended.[2]

When President Kimball became the prophet in 1974, he was widely known for his humility. Once he commented that he thought the Lord had made a mistake in calling him to be president, "unless he knew that I didn't have any sense and would just keep on working." He insisted: "There are many, many men greater than I who could have done a better job."[3] In fact, there may have been many people who privately agreed with that assessment at the outset of his administration. The charismatic, forceful Harold B. Lee had seemed indomitable, and his abbreviated tenure was almost unbelievable. On the other hand, President Kimball seemed physically frail. He had undergone open-heart surgery only one year previous to assuming the mantle of the prophet. Four years earlier he had lost one vocal cord and part of the other to cancer of the throat. Since then, he spoke with great difficulty. Many people foresaw a stalled period in Church history, under a caretaker administration.

In an October 1977 general conference address, Elder William Grant Bangerter of the First Quorum of the Seventy looked back on those difficult days. He described a period of malaise among the Saints as they mourned the loss of President Lee and struggled to accept the new prophet. "We knew, of course, that he would manage somehow, until the next great leader arose, but it would not be easy for him, and things would not be the same. 'O Lord,' we prayed, 'please bless President Kimball. He needs all the help you can give him.'"

According to Elder Bangerter, all of that changed miraculously on April 4, 1974, when a new awareness fell on the General Authorities and the regional representatives of the Church as they listened to a moving address by President Kimball:

"We became alert to an astonishing spiritual presence, and we realized that we were listening to something unusual, powerful, different from any of our previous meetings. It was as if, spiritually speaking, our hair began to stand on end. Our minds were suddenly vibrant and marveling at the transcendent message that was coming to our ears. With a new perceptiveness we realized that President Kimball was opening spiritual windows and beckoning to us to come and gaze with him on the plans of eternity. It was as if he were drawing back the curtains which covered the purpose of the Almighty and inviting us to view with him the destiny of the gospel and the vision of its ministry.

"I doubt that any person present that day will ever forget the occasion. . . . The Spirit of the Lord was upon President Kimball and it proceeded from him to us as a tangible presence, which was at once both moving and shocking. He unrolled to our view a glorious vision. He told us of the ministry performed by the apostles under Joseph Smith. He demonstrated how these men had gone forth in faith and devotion and were clothed with great power, by which they had carried the gospel to the ends of the earth, reaching further, in some ways, than we with the strength of this modern church are doing at the present time. He showed us how the Church was not fully living in the faithfulness that the Lord expects of His people, and that, to a certain degree, we had settled into a spirit of complacency and satisfaction with things as they were. It was at that moment that he sounded the now famous slogan, 'We must lengthen our stride.'"[4]

Spencer W. Kimball, who seemed too humble and too physically weak and small for convincing leadership, was transformed into one of our most effective prophets. His leadership epitomized the desirable balance between confidence and humility. Every leader should be humble and approachable enough to inspire people to identify with him or her, and yet be confident and assertive enough to lead people effectively.

Undoubtedly, every great leader has experienced fear, yet most manage to face it quietly enough that they project only confidence and assurance to followers. Once, when I was a college student, my father and I felt close to panic when my mother suffered a severe nosebleed during the night. Since the bleeding would not stop, I called a physician and arranged to meet him at his office. As Dad and I drove Mom to his office, we felt increasingly confident that someone with knowledge would be caring for her. Surprisingly, the doctor seemed more nervous than we were. He was apparently unnerved by the continued bleeding. He began to cauterize her nose to seal the vessel, but all the while snapped at her with impatience and anxiety that I had never before seen in a physician. Even though his reaction was a very human one, exemplifying his own fears, it caused us to lose confidence in him. We worried that he may not have had enough knowledge to cope with the situation, and we wondered if his emotional reactions would cause him to make a mistake in judgment.

Since then I have thought a great deal about the impact of fear on anyone in the midst of crisis, and I am convinced that however much fear we may experience, we owe it to those who rely on us to exhibit self-assurance. Brigham Young acted as one of the great colonizers of the American West in leading the Mormon pioneers across the plains; yet he faced a monumental challenge for which he was essentially unprepared. While he undoubtedly experienced fears, he always gave the appearance of control and confidence to his followers.

Our ward had a Gospel Doctrine teacher who was especially impressive. She was remarkably well organized, obviously very knowledgeable, and she stimulated us to think and exercise faith. Many times I marveled at her composure and preparation. People who visited the ward invariably commented on our very interesting and inspiring Gospel Doctrine teacher. Several months later when she was a guest in our home she revealed frankly some of her insecurities and fears about her teaching. When we told her how impressed we were with her style and success, she seemed genuinely surprised. She told of an educational conference she had been asked to direct in another state and expressed her frank concerns that she might fail to do a good job. We were incredulous because her composure was such an integral part of her leadership; yet her humility made her even more remarkable to us, and more approachable.

Maurine Turley, a counselor in the general Young Women presidency, told a relevant experience of her own: "When I was a small girl I often played with a friend whose family owned a farm. Her brothers had dug tunnels through stacks of hay in the barn. The tunnels wound in many directions and were dark and frightening. If you made it from one end to the other, you were considered courageous.

"I remember forcing myself through the tunnel opening with heart pounding, very much afraid. I recall crawling for long anxious minutes as I inched myself through the crunchy, stiff hay.

"As I neared the end of the tunnel, suddenly light would burst before me, and I would frantically stretch and reach for the opening at the far end. I gasped the fresh air, relieved to be safe. Overcoming something that frightened me made me feel good about myself. I thought I was absolutely wonderful.

"We all seem to have those tunnels facing us at one time or another. To some people, it's not being popular or slender or a great athlete. Others feel like they don't fit in at school or church. Others might just feel down on themselves and not really know why.

"The important thing is to keep reaching out, to be determined to find the light at the end of your tunnel. It takes a lot of courage, and that's where the gospel can help you. When you know that the spirit within you is the offspring of God—a God who loves you beyond your understanding—and that he supports you all the way, you'll find the light to help you through those tunnels."[5]

When our stake was divided a few years ago, I was called by the new stake president to meet him in his office. Wasting no words, he said, "We would like to call you to be the bishop of the Hingham Ward." I was stunned. I was given one week to pray about the selection of counselors, and I spent that week in a suspended state of fear. Every time the phone rang, I was sure it was a problem I could not solve. It seemed that there was an inordinate number of crises in that first week, when I could deal with them least effectively. Nevertheless, I had to act decisively to bring comfort and advice to the distressed. I learned quickly that regardless of my own fears, I had to *seem* like a bishop who knew what he was doing. One member of the ward must have sensed my insecurities, because after one sacrament meeting she playfully posed this question: "Why were you sitting up there impersonating the bishop?" It was an incisive comment. It was exactly the way I felt. I had to work very hard to try to exude the confidence that others were expecting of me.

At the same time, we should avoid making lengthy and awkward public apologies for what we regard as our inadequacies. Many people are in the habit of spending the first five minutes of a talk or lesson explaining why they are unqualified to be doing it. In the meantime, the minds of the congregation have already started to drift to other subjects, convinced that there is no need to give attention to an unprepared or unqualified speaker. If we are really inadequate, our followers or listeners will discover it soon enough without our telling them. Our time is better spent utilizing our talents in the best way we can to provide effective leadership. The more effort we expend the more effective we will become.

There have been many times with my own children when I needed to exhibit a similar self-assurance. One Christmas day when our two oldest children were very small, Marti and I piled them into the car and traveled to Washington, D.C. to spend the holiday with my sister and her family. Unfortunately, the weather took a nasty turn, and before we reached the New Jersey Turnpike, snow began falling in earnest. As we traveled the turnpike, the blinking speed limit signs continued to signal lower and lower speeds until we were virtually crawling along in the blinding storm. We knew we would not arrive at our destination in time for Christmas dinner, but our children were unconcerned. They were excited about the beautiful snow, and they laughed and talked about it constantly. In the meantime, Marti and I became deeply worried. Washington retains the reputation of having so little snow in winter that city fathers are slow in dealing with it. I kept passing motels and wondering if we should exit and stay the night, but we kept driving and hoping that the storm would subside. For our children's sake, we realized that we had to exhibit optimism and try to conceal our fears that we might be stranded at any time, unable to reach our destination. So we drove carefully, prayed, and talked playfully with the kids.

When we finally reached our exit at one o'clock in the morning on the day *after* Christmas, we were alarmed to find no evidence of tire tracks. There were no other cars and definitely no snowplows in operation. I realized that if

I ever stopped in the deepening snow, I would most certainly not get started again. Miraculously, we successfully negotiated all roads until we finally became stranded on the heavily snowpacked, uphill road on which my sister lived. We left the car and walked the short distance to her house and were greatly relieved to find warmth. To our children the whole thing had been a lark.

Another time we were driving to Utah to visit relatives one summer. In rural Nebraska we drove into the middle of a tornado watch and kept hearing ominous warnings on our car radio. As the sky grew black, we decided to leave the highway and park by a large motel. As we waited there, the clouds began to lift and the threatening storm blew over, the funnel cloud never actually touching down. Through all of this, Marti and I tried to demonstrate a spirit of confidence so that our fears would not be transmitted to our children. There are times when everyone may need to exercise leadership even when feeling terribly inadequate and fearful inside. We may not be able to mask all signs of fear, but with the Lord's help we can develop enough assurance to see us through crises.

Parents also need to be sincerely humble, or teachable, to be effective leaders. They should be willing to acknowledge ignorance or error or admit failure to their children without feeling like they will lose face. Children will come to understand that their parents are human and fallible, and thus respect them more. Parents who are determined to prove that they are in the right in every situation will be found out by their children, and respect will waver. Children will develop more confidence in their parents if they see them as sincere people who are continually working to learn and improve.

There are leaders who feel that because of their position they should never admit that they do not know something. As a result, they may mislead followers or students in a misguided attempt to protect an image. Most people will have greater respect and regard for leaders who will admit to human qualities. If my children ask for my help on a mathematical problem I will try to deal with it, but if it is evident that my knowledge is inadequate, I admit it and send them to Marti. There are even historical questions that I find myself unable to answer, but I can usually guide them to the appropriate source. Every would be leader should be willing to say "I don't know." More important than absolute knowledge is evidence of humility.

I have a brother-in-law who has excelled at everything he has attempted, even though muscular dystrophy has limited his physical accomplishments. He is a highly successful economist, a former bishop, and an energetic father. In all of these activities, he is perceived as determined and dynamic, a man who can set an agenda that people want to follow. He is absolutely confident about his faith in the gospel and everyone senses that immediately, giving them immense confidence in his judgment. Yet he is approachable, with a ready wit and an easy laugh, a man who can almost jokingly persuade people to do what he prefers them to do. His son once told me that there were only two things that his dad considered essential for his children to accomplish: "Go on a mission and keep the lawn cut."Although said in jest, this statement effectively clarifies the range of his father's interests and abilities to influence his children. Even when he is very serious about what he wants them to accomplish, he is able to win their sincere affection through a combination of confidence and humility.

When our family went camping recently in a Massachusetts state forest, we took with us a friend of our twelve-year-old son, David. Josh was an excellent camping companion. He was optimistic and resilient even through a driving rain storm that caused our tent to leak and a mishap the next day that resulted in a broken fishing pole. It occurred to me that not only was he a naturally appealing personality, but he must have had some very effective leadership in the home. I noticed that he almost constantly talked in very positive tones about his father. When he broke his pole, he was disappointed but not hopelessly frustrated. He assured us that his father had a "kit for fixing fishing poles," and he was confident that when he got home it could be repaired. He remembered a night when his father had difficulty changing a tire and had used unusual ingenuity to find an instrument to give him the leverage he lacked. His dad, he said, had a strange talent for finding uses for things that had been discarded by others. In conversation he displayed a reverential attitude toward his father and what he had taught him. This was very interesting to me, because I knew his father well. He had always impressed me most for his humble, unassuming manner. His son knows him better than I do, and he sees a self-confident, approachable man with a penchant for leadership.

In our ward, we had a Young Women's president who maintained just the right balance of confidence and humility. She had an infectious enthusiasm for any project she attempted and an outgoing personality that made her endearing to both young people and adults. She was definitely not shy and seemed most expert in talking with young women about their problems or with parents about their aspirations. Yet she always presented herself as a teachable person who did not know enough and wanted to learn from others. The young women loved her because they were convinced that she was interested in all of them individually. Once, she called my daughter on the phone and asked her to give a talk. Kelly immediately accepted. Impressed with her willingness to do it, the Young Women's president asked her, out of curiosity, why she agreed so readily. Kelly replied, "Because I love you and want to please you." When I overheard my daughter's end of that conversation, I knew that her leader had established a most unusual rapport. The other young women in the ward have made no secret of their willingness to trust her and confide in her.

One of the most challenging assignments for any leader is to be an effective Scoutmaster. Our Scoutmaster is unusually sensitive to Scouting requirements and to the abilities of the boys; he quietly and consistently inspires them to achieve the very highest rank of Eagle. Since he became Scoutmaster, we have had an impressive number of Eagle Scouts, attesting to his dedication and ability to relate to each boy. Any Scoutmaster must be able to inspire the confidence of both parent and boy so that each can trust his leadership in a variety of situations. Our Scoutmaster is assertive and frank with both the boys and the parents and therefore commands respect. Yet, he is also capable of being sensitive to the needs of each boy, which he ascertains in private interviews and as he mingles with them on trips. Once he understands those needs he protects them vigorously, prods each one lightheartedly, and follows their projects through to completion. He is at once assertive and authoritative when he needs to be, and yet humble and spiritual when he needs to be, often expressing heartfelt emotion when talking of their accomplishments.

In one ward, we had a series of ineffective mission leaders, most of whom were hesitant to engage in missionary work and constantly worried that they might offend. When we got a mission leader with a super-salesman spirit, some cynically suspected that it was better to be ineffective. They longed for those men who just came to meetings and required nothing of them. Reacting to the super-salesman who seemed offensive in his techniques and devoted to high-pressure styles, many people became more distressed at the thought of missionary work than ever before. Yet some reasoned that this man with his dynamic and forceful style may have been exactly what was needed. Both groups became so worried about him that missionary work came to a standstill. No one would do it any more because of a distrust and an embarrassment about the mission leader.

This mission leader was later replaced by a man who was determined to do his duty, who was experienced in missionary methods and doctrine, but who insisted on being low-key. He was always quiet and dignified, yet radiated a definite warmth and confidence. People were happy to support him and do what he asked of them. Although the numbers of baptisms did not increase dramatically, the work became productive again and people began to join the Church. Members participated freely, attended baptismal services, and mingled with new members. The new leader unquestionably maintained an impressive balance between confidence and humility.

One of the most important tasks in the Church is home teaching. There was a time in my stake when not one ward had succeeded in having home teachers visit every home once a month. Then an unassuming, inexperienced new convert became an elders quorum president. The ward was famous for its transience, and people with little or no experience were frequently catapulted into top leadership roles. This man was successful in his profession, but he was not considered dynamic by other Church members. Almost overnight, he organized home teaching in the ward more effectively than it had ever been organized before and told the members of his intent to have home teachers visit every home in the ward *at least* once a month. He was not interested in a single glorious month, but rather in a consistent pattern of all home teachers visiting every member of the ward. Most people thought it impossible, and some people laughed at the plan. They waited for him to realize that some people will procrastinate until it is too late, and some people are impossible to find at home. Their cynicism was not rewarded.

Over the new few months, the ward moved gradually upward in home teaching visits until they actually accomplished one hundred percent. There was appropriate fanfare in leadership meetings, and then it was assumed that this was a fluke that would never repeat itself. This elders quorum president managed to accomplish the same feat month after month, until his ward became a standard for home teaching in the stake. There was no magical plan, just a resolute, approachable man who kept close touch with all home teachers and with the families in the ward. He was respected and capable but humble and unassuming, and people responded to his style of leadership. Some time later, he became bishop of the ward.

Carol Lynn Pearson has said, "Our days on this earth will one day be over. All around us are trays heaped with the good things of life. As long as we're here, let's make the most of it. Let's not just browse. Or just sit. There's too much to miss out on. Let's keep in mind the scripture, 'For what doth it profit a man if a gift is bestowed upon him, and he receive not the gift?' (D&C 88:33.) And remember— never, never go into Winchell's without getting a doughnut!"[6]

Leadership of any kind is most effective if the delicate balance is maintained between confidence and humility, between dynamic leadership and feelings of inadequacy. As long as we do not allow it to overcome us, fear can act as a leaven to lift our confidence, a reminder that we are human and vulnerable to error. If we can lead so as to remind our followers that we are aware of our own fallibility yet still have courage to pursue credible goals, we will succeed.

It should be remembered, nevertheless, that arrogance and egocentricity will often drive people away, while confident, self-assured leadership will inspire people to follow. A leader should never forget that the best accomplishments come through gaining the confidence and encouragement of followers. There is very little room for arrogance, but unlimited space for humility.

Chapter Four

THE DANGERS
OF PRIDE

Allegedly there was a bishop who died in Santa Clara, Utah, in the early days of the Church. It was some time before the brethren got around to reorganizing the bishopric. One of the converts, an immigrant, got up in sacrament meeting and said, "Bredren und Sistern, Vat ve need here in dis vard iss a bishop. Und da kind off man ve need for bishop iss a man who doesn't vant to be bishop. Bredren und Sistern, I am here to tell you I doesn't vant to be bishop."[1]

As Latter-day Saints, we believe that it is wrong to aspire to any calling in the Church, because it suggests that we have allowed pride to get in the way of humility. President Kimball once said jokingly to his family, "If I had known it was going to be like this, I would never have run for the office."[2] Because President Kimball was widely recognized as a humble person, he could get away with such a remark, but there are occasionally people who try to use public relations maneuvers in order to achieve Church leadership positions. They may cultivate certain friendships in order to be noticed and perceived as viable leaders. They may show preferential treatment toward people already in leadership roles who might be inclined to call them to key positions. They may perform well in their present positions "to be seen of men" so they will be given higher responsibility. With the Spirit of the Lord, we can avoid being victimized by such an approach. For the good of the Church and for all its members, people should not be

42

encouraged to use techniques within the Church that are guaranteed to help them climb the corporate ladder.

One of the best examples of humility toward church callings is found in the life of Spencer W. Kimball. While a successful businessman in Arizona in 1943, Elder Kimball received a phone call from J. Reuben Clark, a member of the First Presidency. President Clark told him that he had been selected to fill a vacancy in the Quorum of the Twelve Apostles. Elder Kimball's reply was: "Oh, Brother Clark! Not me. You don't mean me. There must be some mistake. I surely couldn't have heard you right." Then he sank past the chair to the floor. President Clark assured him that the call was legitimate. Elder Kimball broke out in a sweat, caught his breath, and looked at a "complete panorama" of the little, mean, petty things he thought he had done. He felt unworthy for such a call and shrank from it. When he hung up the phone he told his wife, "They have called me to become an apostle." Sister Kimball's response was, "Are you sure that you were to be an apostle?" "No, I am not sure now," said this humble man who was destined to become the prophet.[3] Clearly, his humility was his strongest recommendation to serve both as an apostle and as president of the Church.

President J. Reuben Clark, Jr., who issued that call, also had occasion to demonstrate a spirit of humility and the absence of pride in connection with his long career of Church administration. At the time he was called to be a General Authority, he had served only as a Sunday School teacher and an auxiliary board member. When a rumor surfaced among his friends in 1931 that he would be called as an apostle, he said, "I think there is no more danger of my being named an apostle than there is of my flying to the moon. I have never sought or craved church office."[4] Actually, the rumor was not quite correct. President Heber J. Grant wanted Brother Clark to become his counselor in the First Presidency, where he served from 1934 until 1951.

When George Albert Smith died and David O. McKay

became President in 1951, President McKay called Elder Stephen L Richards, who had more than seventeen years seniority over President Clark, as his first counselor, and made President Clark his second counselor. To make it more difficult, President Clark was asked by President McKay to present the new First Presidency to the general conference for the sustaining vote. This was said to have been an electrifying moment in general conference history, but J. Reuben Clark presented the names without a trace of personal emotion. Afterwards, President McKay explained that apostolic seniority was the reason for the change, and not any rift between the brethren, and that it was in no way a demotion. Then he called on President Clark to speak before President Richards. President Clark's impressive and heartfelt statement during his address was, "In the service of the Lord, it is not where you serve but how. In The Church of Jesus Christ of Latter-day Saints, one takes the place to which one is duly called, which place one neither seeks nor declines."[5]

The scriptural warnings against pride are legion. Nephi complained that people often became "puffed up in their hearts." He noted that "because of pride," churches became corrupted. Some people wore "stiff necks and high heads" and because of pride they committed acts of wickedness. He observed that the wise and the learned and the rich "are puffed up in the pride of their hearts." (See 2 Nephi 28:9-16.) Helaman complained that the people "set their hearts upon the vain things of the world."

"Yea, how quick to be lifted up in pride; yea, how quick to boast, and do all manner of that which is iniquity; and how slow are they to remember the Lord their God, and to give ear unto his counsels, yea, how slow to walk in wisdom's path!" (Helaman 12:5.)

And for Latter-day Saints, a classic scripture is found in the Doctrine and Covenants, when the Lord outlined the dangers of pride to Joseph Smith: "Because their hearts are set so much upon the things of this world, and aspire to the honors of men, that they do not learn this one lesson—that the rights of the priesthood are inseparably connected with the powers of heaven, and that the powers of heaven cannot be controlled nor handled only upon the principles of righteousness.

"That they may be conferred upon us, it is true; but when we undertake to cover our sins, or to gratify our pride, our vain ambition, or to exercise control or dominion or compulsion upon the souls of the children of men, in any degree of unrighteousness, behold, the heavens withdraw themselves; the Spirit of the Lord is grieved; and when it is withdrawn, Amen to the priesthood or the authority of that man. . . .

"We have learned by sad experience that it is the nature and disposition of almost all men, as soon as they get a little authority, as they suppose, they will immediately begin to exercise unrighteous dominion. Hence many are called, but few are chosen." (D&C 121:35-40.)

We would never have received such strong advice if we were not to be consistently tempted by pride. We should be cautious and avoid the tendencies to embrace pride in leadership. Throughout the early history of the Church there were problems or conflicts having their origins in pride. Such illustrious leaders as Orson Pratt, Amasa Lyman, Orson Hyde, Thomas B. Marsh, Oliver Cowdery, Sidney Rigdon, Martin Harris, and David Whitmer suffered some of the effects of pride, climaxed by their leaving the Church. There were cases of insubordination regarding the leadership of Joseph Smith and criticism of Church leaders. One of the more interesting cases involved Thomas B. Marsh, the president of the Quorum of the Twelve Aspostles. In 1838, a Church court ruled against President Marsh's wife in a dispute over milk strippings. According to Elder George A. Smith, this is what happened:

"When the saints were living in Far West, the wife of Marsh and Sister Harris (wife of George Washington Har-

ris) agreed to exchange milk, in order to enable each of
them to make a larger cheese than they could do sepa-
rately. Each was to take the other the "strippings" as well
as the rest of the milk. Mrs. Harrris performed her part of
the agreement, but Mrs. Marsh kept a pint of "strippings"
from each cow. When this became known the matter was
brought before the Teachers, and these decided against
Mrs. Marsh. An appeal was taken to the Bishop. He sustained the Teachers. If Marsh had obeyed the Revelation
and governed his house in humility and with steadfast-
ness, he would have righted the wrong done, but instead
of doing so, he appealed to the High Council. Marsh, who
at the time was President of the Twelve, possibly thought
that the Council would favor him, but that body confirmed
the Bishop's decision. He was not yet satisfied, but appealed to the First Presidency, and Joseph, the Prophet,
and his two Counselors consented to review the case. They
approved the finding of the High Council. Was Marsh
satisfied then? No. With the persistency of Lucifer himself,
he declared that he would uphold the character of his wife,
'even if he had to go to hell for it.'"[6]

In 1856, Thomas Marsh had a change of heart after suffering a stroke. "Look at me," he said to the Saints at
Winter Quarters, "and see the results of apostasy; had I
been faithful to my calling as the President of the Twelve, I
would now occupy the position that Brigham Young does,
as President of the Church."[7] He was rebaptized on the
journey West. Later, he spoke to the assembled Saints in
Salt Lake City at the invitation of Brigham Young:

"He loved me too much to let me go without whipping.
I have seen the hand of the Lord in the chastisement which
I have received. I have seen and know that it has proved
that he loved me; for if he had not cared anything about
me, he would not have taken me by the arms and given me
such a shaking . . . Many have said to me 'how is it that a
man like you, who understood so much of the revelations
of God as recorded in the Book of Doctrine and Covenants,

should fall away?' I told them not to feel too secure, but to take heed lest they should also fall; for I had no scruples in my mind as to the possibility of men falling away. . . . You will not then think nor feel for a moment as you did before you lost the Spirit of Christ for when men apostatize, they are left to grovel in the dark. . . . I have frequently wanted to know how my apostacy began, and I have come to the conclusion that I have lost the Spirit of the Lord out of my heart."[8]

He also expressed a true spirit of repentance and asked the members to accept him: "I have come here to get good society—to get your fellowship; I want your God to be my God, and I want to live with you forever, in time and eternity. I never want to forsake the people of God anymore. I want to have your confidence, and I want to be one in the house of God."[9]

If such a serious problem could change the entire life of the man who would have been president of the Church, then it can affect any of us as well. Yet we sometimes notice examples of the opposite extreme. The man who eventually became my stake president moved into our ward several years ago while cultivating purposely what he called a "low profile." He was happy, he said, attending meetings and soaking up messages from the pulpit. He was willing to serve, but had no desire to hold leadership positions. Soon he was called as Sunday School president where he remained very unassuming, but his desired anonymity was not to be. Only a few months afterward he was called to be the bishop of the ward, and three years later, the stake president. Clearly, his low profile technique did not produce the expected results. Recently, another young man moved into our ward with a similar desire. He sat on the back row and seemed perfectly contented to be ignored or even forgotten. Within a matter of weeks he was called to be a counselor in the bishopric.

Similarly, one of the most soft-spoken women in our ward was called as the Relief Society president. Although she was stunned, she immediately thrust herself into the calling with impressive faith and ability. It may be that the Lord approves of the sincerely low profile person and rewards the humility exemplified with opportunities for leadership. A humble person devoid of ambition for callings is less likely to exploit his or her leadership position for reasons of personal advantage.

It is undesirable for persons who serve in the Church to allow callings or positions to become proprietorships rather than stewardships. Sometimes the tendencies to become such develop through longevity in office. All leaders are most effective when they are willing to take suggestions, willing to recognize faults, and willing to give credit for accomplishments to the Lord and the many others who serve Him. It is also undesirable for leaders to take advantage of their positions to unfairly criticize those they serve.

In our homes we should avoid the temptation to speak ill of various ward members, thus making a lasting impression on our children. If we have a prejudice against certain members or leaders, we owe it to our children to keep it to ourselves. To poison their minds against someone because of our own personal experience is unfair to a person who may have changed and to our children who may have different inclinations in friendship. My brother-in-law always says, "I don't care what we discuss at dinner, as long as we don't criticize the brethren in front of the children." This is an old adage in many Mormon homes, and it is a good one. It is unfair to those people we lead to leave them with our own negative images of people.

Parents may be tempted to engage in theatrics as they assert authority in the home. They may feel threatened if children disagree with a family policy and therefore make statements that overemphasize their leadership position. They may feel threatened by any perceived failure of their children to show them proper respect. Although parents, especially of very young children, need to teach respect for authority, they need also to demonstrate rapport with their children. Most fathers would not be happy with a child who insisted on calling him by his first name, but he need not show the same sense of authority if the child makes a lighthearted comment following serious parental pronouncements. A wise parent can appreciate the humor in the comment without embracing the message. Overreaction usually opens rifts that need not even exist. An open channel of communication can be maintained without relying on authoritarian techniques exclusively.

I was a guest at a family home evening conducted by a well-meaning father. After he began to discuss some family business, there were several funny comments made by the children that I thought were genuinely funny, but harmless. The father was not amused and interpreted the comments as intentional efforts to undermine his authority. Stiffly, he reprimanded the entire group for their demeanor until there was a chill in the air.

Through the rest of the evening, members of the family responded briefly and awkwardly to questions, making it virtually impossible to have a productive discussion. Authority had been preserved, but the atmosphere was destroyed. Respect, such as it was, came at a heavy cost.

The opposite was true in a home evening we shared with another family. We had a short lesson in which my sons David and Charlie presented some important points that were followed by some additional comments from me. The spirit was light, but all were attentive. There was humor, but it was well received. The lesson and games were divided among several people, thus diffusing authority but preserving organization. It was an equal and successful arrangement.

As Primary president, Joan was very businesslike and dedicated to her work, but also seemingly very insecure about her authority. At presidency meetings, she was serious in the extreme and authoritarian to the point of taking the joy out of the work for both of her counselors. She carefully parceled out the work to her counselors, then called numerous times to follow up, not hesitating to angrily reprove for work not yet done. At times, she seemed more interested in the authority of her calling than in the task itself.

In another ward, Marjorie was Primary president and seemed the epitome of wisdom. To her teachers she always offered her time and support, but never exerted her authority unnecessarily. Conversely, she was most inclined toward praising for what she considered a job well done. After sitting in on a class, she was quick to talk enthusiastically about the lesson material and the examples she thought particularly effective. "You're a master teacher!" she would often say. She was seemingly secure in her own accomplishments in life, not hungry for acclaim but only desirous of helping and encouraging others. She felt no need to use her Church position to put people in their places or to underline her own authority. Those who served under her loved her and felt inspired to do better.

People in any position of leadership may be tempted to exploit the position and the people they are serving. The expressed desire to put someone in his place or the exploitation of temper in order to teach someone a lesson are clearly out of place in Church leadership. Leadership in the Church should always be characterized by humility, gentleness of manner, and sincerity without deceit. Any leader experiences times when righteous indignation may be called for, as when Jesus ordered the money changers out of the temple, but anger must be used carefully and righteously. A leader who feels the need to show position, power, or influence to someone else is in fact an insecure person exhibiting selfishness rather than righteous anger.

We are, perhaps, most tempted to exhibit anger during our leadership in the home. Every time I have allowed anger to push out reason in my relationships with my children, I have regretted it. One weekend while Marti was away, I was acting as a single parent with more pressures than usual. On Sunday morning we felt rushed, and by the time we all climbed in the car to head for Church, we were running late. It was my own fault. I had tried to do too many things in the last few minutes, and I became impatient with my children, who were actually doing remarkably well. After we had driven for about five minutes, I remembered that I had left some materials at home that I had promised Marti I would deliver to the Church. When I turned around to go retrieve them, two of my sons persisted in making cynical comments about how this trip would insure our tardiness. Back in our own driveway, one of them estimated the exact number of minutes the trip back was costing us, and how many minutes late we would be to Church as a result. I exploded. "The next person who makes a comment about how late we are going to be," I said in a self-righteous burst of energy, "is *dead!*" I allowed a tiny problem to arouse my anger and cause me to make a thoughtless comment, even though it could undermine my leadership in the home. By doing it on the way to Church, I also endangered the Spirit of the Sabbath day for my children. Although I was immediately sorry and apologized, my children remembered the incident well enough to describe it in copious detail to Marti when she returned that evening.

We should make every effort to curb anger, never using it to show our authority or to manipulate people. Persons with pride are those most tempted to manipulate their followers instead of lead them. It is the same mentality that teaches us that we can get what we want in life by using charisma on people, by complimenting them at crucial times, by using cheap techniques to persuade them to do what we want them to do. Many best-selling self-help books are based on the art of personal manipulation. Readers are advised to massage self-esteem by hypocritically admiring people's children or homes or even their dogs.

According to James MacGregor Burns, this technique is false leadership, because it is selfish and personal. "Fully sharing leaders perceive their roles as shaping the future to the advantage of groups with which they identify, an ad-

vantage they define in terms of the broadest possible goals
and the highest possible levels of morality. Leaders are
taskmasters and goal setters, but they and their followers
share a particular space and time, a particular set of motivations and values. If they are to be effective in helping to
mobilize their constituencies, leaders must be whole persons, persons with fully functioning capacities for thinking
and feeling. The problem for them as educators, as leaders,
is not to promote narrow, egocentric self-actualization but
to extend awareness of human needs and the means of
gratifying them, to improve the larger social situation for
which educators or leaders have responsibility and over
which they have power. Is it too much to believe that it is
'the grand goal of all leadership—to help create or maintain
the social harbors for these personal islands?'"[10]

Personal manipulation and "egocentric self-actualization" are inconsistent with effective leadership. They are
motivated by love of self and personal ambitions instead of
love of followers and service. Effective leaders should constantly be on the alert for signs of pride that will undermine
their relationship with others and cause the quality of their
service to be harmed.

An effective leader is the kind of person who is comfortable serving, without any need for someone else to recognize his supposed importance. Jesus washed his apostles'
feet and said, "He that is greatest among you shall be your
servant."

Chapter Five

REPROVING WITH LOVE

Even Jesus found it necessary at times to reprove for righteous reasons. For instance, he was disturbed by the presence of moneychangers in the temple: "They come to Jerusalem: and Jesus went into the temple, and began to cast out them that sold and bought in the temple, and overthrew the tables of the moneychangers, and the seats of them that sold doves; and would not suffer that any man should carry any vessel through the temple. And he taught, saying unto them, Is it not written, My house shall be called of all nations the house of prayer? but ye have made it a den of thieves. And the scribes and chief priests heard it, and sought how they might destroy him: for they feared him, because all the people was astonished at his doctrine." (Mark 11:15-19.)

Similarly, he reproved the Pharisees for living lives of hypocrisy. "Even so ye also outwardly appear righteous unto men, but within ye are full of hypocrisy and iniquity." (Matthew 23:28.) Jesus even reproved his disciples in the Garden of Gethsemane when he poured out his heart to his Father and then found his disciples asleep. "What, could ye not watch with me one hour? Watch and pray, that ye enter not into temptation." But he always demonstrated compassion afterwards, as when he added that "the spirit indeed is willing, but the flesh is weak." (Matthew 26:40-41.)

We may have the need to speak directly or sharply in carrying out our responsibilities, but we must remember to show greater love afterwards, as indicated by this advice from the Lord: "No power or influence can or ought to be maintained by virtue of the priesthood, only by persuasion, by long-suffering, by gentleness and meekness, and by love unfeigned; by kindness, and pure knowledge, which shall greatly enlarge the soul without hypocrisy, and without guile—

"Reproving betimes with sharpness, when moved upon by the Holy Ghost; and then showing forth afterwards an increase of love toward him whom thou hast reproved, lest he esteem thee to be his enemy." (D&C 121:41-43.)

In the history of the Church, Brigham Young is one of the most obvious examples of reproving with sharpness; he was a leader who often spoke directly. In a sermon given at the Bowery in Salt Lake City, August 17, 1856, President Young said:

"When I rise before you, brethren and sisters, I often speak of the faults of the people and try to correct them; I strive to put the Saints in a right course and plead with them to live their religion, to become better and to purify themselves before the Lord; . . . I am always ready to impart what I have to this people, that which will cheer and comfort their hearts, and if the Lord will lead me by His Spirit into that train of reflections and teaching, I am more willing and ready to speak comforting words to this people, than I am to chastise them.

"But I hope and trust in the Lord my God that I shall never be left to praise this people, to speak well of them, for the purpose of cheering and comforting them by the art of flattery; to lead them on by smooth speeches day after day, week after week, month after month, and year after year, and let them roll sin as a sweet morsel under their tongues, and be guilty of transgressing the law of God. I hope I shall never be left to flatter this people, or any people on the earth, in their iniquity, but far rather chasten them for their wickedness and praise them for their godliness."[1]

President Young practiced what he preached in many different instances, especially during the great migration of Mormon pioneers westward. Once, the company Parley P. Pratt was leading had been organized incorrectly. According to Thomas Bullock, "Prest. Young reproved P.P.P. very strongly for disorganizing all the Winter's work of the Quorum of the Twelve. He at his first manifested a contra Spirit, but afterwards repented—the Spirit and power of God was poured out—much instruction was given—and it proved a most glorious meeting to all."[2]

In his autobiography, Parley P. Pratt said that he had deserved the chastisement, that he asked forgiveness and was frankly forgiven: "This school of experience made me humble and careful in the future, and I think it was the means of making me a wiser and better man ever after."[3]

Brigham Young realized that he had a tendency to harshness with people. In a speech in 1853, he said, "Never, in the days of my life, have I hurt a man with the palm of my hand. I never have hurt a person any other way except with this unruly member, my tongue."[4] Yet other early Church presidents believed in chastisement, and in general, Brigham Young's use of it. John Taylor, third president of the Church, warned bishops not to "cover up the iniquities of men." In suggesting that leaders needed to call others to repentance, he warned that any who failed to meet that challenge would bear the burden of the sins of others. "Do you hear it, you Bishops and you Presidents? God will require it at your hands. You are not placed in a position to tamper with the principles of righteousness, nor to cover up the infamies and corruptions of men."[5]

Wilford Woodruff, who became the fourth president, also supported the concept and defended Brigham Young's habit of chastising the members, saying that it was for their good. "Do I blame President Young because he chastises us? No. Would he be a father to us, a Prophet, and a High Priest of God, if he saw his brethren going wrong, and would not warn and chastise them? The chastisement of a friend is far better than the kisses of an enemy. When I am out of the way, and when you are out of the way, I thank God that we have a man to preside over us, who loves us enough to chastise us; it is for our good, and I believe we have been always ready to receive the chastening rod from our superiors when they thought fit to give it to us, and kiss the rod that chastened us. . . . The very spirit that vibrates in the soul of President Young, and every act of his life, show, to all acquainted with him, that he will do his duty in this respect. . . . The Lord has reproved the wicked in all ages, and He will do it again."[6]

A good example of such reproof is found in Doctrine and Covenants 19:15, when the Lord said to Martin Harris, "I command you to repent—repent, lest I smite you by the rod of my mouth, and by my wrath, and by my anger, and your sufferings be sore—how sore you know not, how exquisite you know not, yea, how hard to bear you know not." Church leaders may have occasion to reprove members of the ward in a group setting for various reasons. One bishop became concerned that instead of attending Sunday School, ward members were congregating in the halls and sitting in the foyers, talking and transacting church business. Realizing that his own habit of conducting interviews while he expected members to attend Sunday School made him an unconvincing example, he pledged to eliminate all interviews during church meetings and attend Sunday School himself. Then he encouraged the other members of the ward to attend with him. Attendance took a dramatic rise the first week, then dipped again, and so he went into the halls and personally solicited people to come.

A Relief Society president reproved members in a meeting for not sacrificing enough for the benefit of the building program; there was a significant change afterward in attitudes toward making financial contributions and toward sacrificing time for the Lord's work. In every case, it is important that leaders be willing to do exactly as they are suggesting that others do.

I once observed a Primary president react with horror

when a ward member grew so impatient that a meeting was running over that he spoke loudly and pounded on the door. This resolute woman opened the door and in firm, even tones, reprimanded the man for disturbing the closing prayer of their meeting. She expressed the hope that he would never do such a thing again and then closed the door. A few minutes later, when people left the room, the man was effusive in his apology for being impulsive and insensitive. He fully realized his error, and she had been effective in reproving him.

Past experience has proven, however, that it is usually wise to avoid exercising reproof toward individuals in a group setting. In teaching my college classes, I sometimes have to admonish students who are talking and thus disturbing the class. Usually, I try to give these students a message with my eyes, and if that fails to work, I ask to see them privately after class. In every case, I have had good results by making it clear that the behavior is unacceptable in class. I tell the students that I chose to discuss it privately so as not to embarrass them publicly, and they appreciate the courtesy. The students usually realize that they were making a disturbance and then agree to improve. But if I had chosen to embarrass the students in class by reproving them publicly, they may have been angry with me and responded with retaliation. Ordinarily, then, private reproof of individuals is the most effective and the most humane practice.

This is equally true in a family setting. If a child persists in disturbing dinner or family home evening by making ill-advised comments, it may be most effective to talk to the child privately. "Steve, let me talk with you for a few minutes privately after dinner." Usually, both Steve and the other children will know that he is about to be reproved, but he will be comforted and grateful to know that all his brothers and sisters will not hear it. It is more likely that the words of reproof will be taken seriously. Private reproof brings increased respect.

A member of the priesthood executive council persisted

in being argumentative with the bishop and others, presenting his views in an abrasive way. The bishop realized that he should call this man in privately, but before he could do so, he allowed his anger to surface in the group and publicly admonished the offending member. Afterwards, he realized that it was the wrong choice, and he tried to correct the error in a private interview. The two were able to come to a meeting of the minds, but an impression had been left with several other people that was difficult to erase.

Occasionally, reproof to a group works in a public setting if it is not entered into too often. Once, I accompanied the young people of my ward to a super-Saturday activity that culminated with a dance. I noticed early in the evening that our group was not having a terribly good time, but I failed to realize its significance. I left the cultural hall for just a few minutes, and when I returned, the only young person remaining from our ward was my own son. He told me that the others had left to go to a movie. I was angry that they would do such a thing without consulting me, and that they would fail to support this stake-sponsored event. On Sunday morning, during the joint meeting we held with the young people, I expressed to them my candid views about what they had done. Essentially, I reproved them, telling them that I never wanted them to do it again. I also made it clear to them that I understood their objections to the activity, and that the event in no way interfered with my love for them. They listened attentively, and some of them responded apologetically. Even given the anger, we were able to discuss it with a touch of humor. Afterward, it seemed that they were respectful and sincerely repentant. It was one of those times when it seemed wise to express anger frankly, rather than letting it pass. If I had constantly blown off steam for numerous offenses, however, it might have been considerably less effective.

I recall a Sunday School teacher I had as a youth. She was a serious, discipline-conscious woman who had trouble relating to the large class of eleven- and twelve-year-olds. She always seemed angry at us for something, and she tried various heavy-handed techniques to get her message across. For example, she instituted two minutes of meditation, during which we would not speak at all, but would concentrate on spiritual things. There was never complete silence when we entered the meditation, and several class members could not resist saying something sarcastic to elicit laughter. We had very little respect for the teacher, and the more she railed at us, the less we seemed to care. When another young man and I were approached by the Sunday School superintendent and asked to be examples by giving the support that this teacher needed, we could not believe it. It seemed to be an admission that this woman could not handle the class. Although we agreed to try to influence others to better behavior, the teacher asked for release soon afterward. Throughout her tenure, she exhibited poor judgment. Reproof must be delivered selectively and carefully enough to elicit respect.

In my experience, children often reprove each other, even when it is undeserved. They sometimes assume that they are wise enough to act in the role of a parent and try to administer discipline to a brother or sister. My younger sons sometimes fall into that trap, and when it happens, we reprove them for reproving each other. One evening they were all having a snack before bedtime while we were out of the room. David noticed that Charlie was not sitting close enough to the table and crumbs were falling on the floor, so he told Charlie to sit closer. Of course, Charlie refused, even though he knew that David was right. He just did not like the order coming from his brother. In anger, David physically pushed Charlie closer to the table, resulting in retaliation from Charlie and disaster for the food they were eating. Charlie allowed his temper to explode, but David put Charlie in a difficult position by playing the parenting role. Both boys needed reproof, but the older one especially needed to understand that it was not his responsibility to administer discipline. Marti and I talked with them about the significance of the problem, trying to help them see that both were in the wrong.

Recently, in a department store, I observed a young father screaming at his tiny daughter, who chased him down the aisle and fell at his feet. Instead of helping her up, he yelled out, "I told you to stop *running!*" Then he went back to looking at clothing displays. Not far behind was his wife who was angry at her husband for what she had just observed. "You *scream* at her for *falling down?*" she asked in desperation, running to the little girl's aid. The father became more angry still. "*Shut up!*" he said to his wife. "I don't want her running in here!"

While this incident may be typical of many people and their tenuous relations with their children, it points to a basic problem. Parents whether angry or not must cling to a rational analysis of the problem, and they must remember that a child is a very important person whose personality and character is being formed partly based on the treatment he is receiving from his parents. This man screamed and exploded in anger, but he did not take time to reprove with thoughtful advice or to show enough love afterward to convince the little girl that he would not be angry with her forever.

Parenting often presents the greatest challenge to principles of leadership because parents are so close to their children that they feel very deeply about them and yet see them so often that they are likely to behave impulsively. Many parents act quickly in anger when dealing with their children. When a parent gets angry, it is especially important to express righteous indignation, to control the expression of temper, and to demonstrate kindness and love afterward. If that is done, the reasons for the reproof will carry much more weight, and the memory children have of their parents will tend to be positive. A careful, rational response is imperative to establishing effective leadership in the home.

Chapter Six

REACHING
THE INDIVIDUAL

A relevant passage from the Doctrine and Covenants concerns the worth of a soul: "Remember the worth of souls is great in the sight of God. . . . Wherefore, you are called to cry repentance unto this people. And if it so be that you should labor all your days in crying repentance unto this people, and bring, save it be one soul unto me, how great shall be your joy with him in the kingdom of my Father!" (D&C 18: 10, 14-15.)

Reaching "the one" becomes, then, a crucial part of the gospel, and every leader should be devoted to the individual. Elder Marion D. Hanks once told the story of an elderly man who walked onto the grounds of Temple Square in Salt Lake City. The man, who was unkempt, unshaven, and reeked of the smell of alcohol and tobacco, made his way to the desk where Elder Hanks, director of the bureau of information, sat. Pointing to the temple, he said, "How do I get in there?" Elder Hanks assumed that he was a tourist and began to explain the purpose and story of temples, when the man stopped him, saying, "Oh, you don't have to tell me all that. I know that. You see, I am a Mormon."

"Well," said Elder Hanks, "if you are a member of the Church and you know all of this, what is it you want from me?" He said, "Frankly, nothing. There isn't anything you have to give me. I am here because my wife insisted on my coming in, but I have fulfilled my errand," and he left.

Later, Elder Hanks noticed the elderly man walking out

on the grounds with a younger woman who proved to be his third wife. Elder Hanks asked the man how he had come to this feeling of antagonism and indifference toward the Church. The man said that at age nineteen he was ejected from a chapel by a bishop's counselor for making a disturbance in Sunday School class. As he was thrown out, someone objected, to which the counselor said in reply, "Ah, let him go. He's just one kid." The man kept this incident in his memory for nearly sixty years.

He left, and he never came back. His third wife, who had been taught the gospel by missionaries, brought him there, to Temple Square, hoping that he might be touched in some way to realize the truthfulness of the gospel. "Now," said Elder Hanks, "this was especially significant: that man had fifty-four living descendants, and not one was a member of the Church! Was it just *one* boy the bishop's counselor propelled out the door that morning? Just one?"[1]

The reverse of that story is found in an account by the late Elder Charles A. Callis. While he was president of the Southern States Mission, a young man who had completed his two years as a missionary came in to see him and make a final report. When President Callis asked him what he had accomplished, his reply was, "President Callis, I have accomplished nothing. I have wasted my time and my father's money, and I'm going home." President Callis asked, "Haven't you had a single baptism?" He said, "Yes, I've had one. I baptized a man in the backwoods where we have only a little Sunday School—a man who doesn't even wear shoes."

President Callis said, "I was intrigued with that young man's sense of failure. When next I went up into that district, I looked up that man. I found he'd put on shoes, that he'd put on a shirt and a tie, that he was secretary of the little branch Sunday School. He became the superintendent of the branch Sunday School. He was ordained a deacon and then a teacher and then a priest and then an elder. He became the president of the branch. He moved off the little tenant farm on which he and his father before him had lived and got a piece of ground and cleared it and made it fruitful. He became the district president. He sold his farm and moved to Idaho, where he developed a fine farm in the Snake River Valley. His boys grew and went on missions, and now his grandsons have gone on missions."

Finally, Charles Callis said, "I've been up in Idaho the past week making a survey, and I've discovered that, as a result of that one baptism by a young man who came home thinking he'd failed, more than eleven hundred people have come into the Church." In the Doctrine and Covenants, the Lord said: "Wherefore, be not weary in well-doing, for ye are laying the foundation of a great work. And out of small things proceedeth that which is great. Behold, the Lord requireth the heart and a willing mind."[2]

Reaching the individual can only be accomplished by establishing close relationships with people. People who become leaders too often feel the need to distance themselves from followers in order to encourage respect. In speaking of Jesus, President Kimball said, "He walked and worked with those he was to serve. His was not a long-distance leadership. He was not afraid of close friendships; he was not afraid that proximity to him would disappoint his followers. The leaven of true leadership cannot lift others unless we are with and serve those to be led."[3]

The bishop of my father's ward initiated a project to assist my father in cutting down dead trees and cleaning up brush and debris on Dad's property. He declared one Saturday to be "Leo Lythgoe Day" and invited the ward members to congregate on the family property and accomplish all they could. It was not only a marvelously successful service project, but it was a genuinely effective way of putting leaders and followers together in work clothes, accomplishing the same worthy purpose together. My dad watched in amazement as numerous people tackled a number of different projects, often with machines, and restored his yard to the meticulous model he had spent almost ninety years cultivating and maintaining.

A former bishop of mine was a highly successful professional whose demanding schedule rarely allowed him to mix with the people outside of his regularly scheduled interviews and church meetings. When we planned a major service project to completely renovate an old home, the bishop planned to be there as well, a fact that shocked but pleased many people. Most had never seen him roll up his sleeves and engage in physical work, or laugh and joke while rubbing shoulders with the members. The project was a very gratifying experience for the large number of people who came and participated, as much for the opportunity of observing their bishop in down-to-earth circumstances as it was for the service rendered. In fact, his presence and active role in the project served as an impetus to many people to give it all of their energy. This newfound respect remained in many people's minds for a long time afterward.

The same bishop also was rarely able to attend youth activities, but one day when our ward was in charge of preparing a dance and refreshments for the stake young people, he put on his tennis shoes and crewneck sweater and played an active role. The young people took to him enthusiastically and enjoyed this new side of their leader. It seemed evident that these casual, unstructured ways of mingling with the people were some of his most meaningful. Many of us wished that his professional responsibilities allowed him to participate in such activities more often.

One Young Women's presidency was so convinced of the importance of getting to know each young woman intimately that they each arranged many different times to be with them in small groups and individually. One volunteered to cut and style my daughter's hair at her home. Another volunteered to take a small group into Boston on a Saturday afternoon for some unstructured fun and conversation. Another invited several of them over to her home for an evening of cooking and enjoying desserts. Then, one at a time, she invited the young women into her home in an effort to know their thoughts and concerns. Few leaders are so dedicated and also so effective. The respect held for these women by those they served was unbounded.

We can apply the same principle to leadership in the home, or virtually any other environment. If parents are always in a position to pontificate and direct activities, without ever participating in them personally, children will not feel close to them. I have found the experience of playing basketball on a weekly basis with my sons to be a marvelous way of getting to know them. We need to be friends with our children and find things to do with them that will allow our relationships to develop without formal organization.

I have noticed the same thing in my professional teaching. Periodically, I have students who are so interested in the subject matter that they come to my office to talk about it informally. Or, I may have a chance to get to know a few students more deeply by directing their honors work, which involves many consultations. One student did his honors work by researching at the John F. Kennedy Library in Boston while I was doing research there myself. We found a mutual bond in the study of political history, and we laughed and talked about a variety of things, causing our relationship to become more meaningful. This student has developed a certain empathy toward me that extends beyond the formal classroom. We now talk in a variety of situations that do not pertain to the academic setting. I may have influenced him more than most of my students.

Another student, a young lady, took all of my courses because she enjoyed the atmosphere in the classroom, then went on to do honors work. She chose to write about the Mormon pioneers, necessitating her direct research in the Church archives in Salt Lake City. She flew there and spent some time before returning to Boston and writing an honors paper for me, which she presented orally to history students and faculty. In the course of this academic work, she developed a sincere interest in the Church. I was careful not to deal with this in an academic setting, but after her honors work was completed, I asked some missionaries to call on her. While she was being taught, she occasionally dropped in to discuss some of the points that the missionaries were explaining. We had some productive gospel discussions, and one day, she asked if I would baptize her. I was elated and went with my family to her ward and officiated at her baptismal service.

Shortly afterward, she went to Brigham Young University to do graduate work, became employed by the genealogical department of the Church, and finally, served a mission to Portugal. I know that I was just in the right place at the right time to assist this outstanding young woman in accepting the gospel, but it seems unlikely that it would have happened had we not become friends outside the formal academic setting.

According to William Dyer, a professor of organizational behavior at Brigham Young University, the "challenge for the leader in any organization, be it business, church, or the family, is to engage in the kinds of actions that will let those who work with him know that he has a vital, personal concern about them as individuals."[4]

Dr. Rensis Likert, formerly of the University of Michigan, stated that the "principle of supportive relationships" is vital for any organization. Every person must view the leadership of the organization as supportive of his own values and expectations in order to benefit his own sense of personal worth.[5] Dr. Dyer believes that within the structure of any organization, it is vital that all assignments and programs are presented with an "overriding concern for those who must do the work and carry out the assignments. When people feel that their superior thinks the work is more important than the people who do it, the motivation to work is hindered."[6]

As an example, Dr. Dyer suggested that when a person is called to a position in the Church, it is important that the human dimension be included. "Is the person who issues the call so intent on covering the nature of the assignment, the requirements, and the importance of the work that he fails to deal with the needs, concerns, fears, and questions of the person being called?"[7] The person issuing the call may expect the person being called to react out of respect for authority or obedience to the gospel. That expectation is really contrary to the nature of the gospel, which is geared to human needs. My wife was once called to serve in the presidency of a Church auxiliary while she lay in a hospital bed, having given birth to a child only hours before. It was assumed that she would accept out of duty, and no apparent consideration was given to her personal needs. I was once called to a position as a Sunday School teacher between meetings while standing outside the Church building on the sidewalk with a member of the bishopric. At the time I thought that since I was not approached in a more personal and private way that the call was not very important, or that the leader did not regard me as very important.

Oral interviews are sometimes conducted by leaders who spend all their time asking about the home teaching families or the organization in question without talking deeply and personally about the concerns of the person being interviewed. Similarly, a bishop doing interviews for temple recommends or tithing settlement may schedule appointments without sufficient time for each person to recognize his genuine concern. Certainly, no leader can get close to people he serves if he does nothing but ask the formal questions in an interview setting.

Dr. Dyer asks, "In church classes, do some teachers make the students feel that the lesson is more important than the learner?" He believes that "it is the wise and skillful teacher who can create a class atmosphere where students can talk about the the real issues and questions they have about the gospel."[8] Some Sunday School teachers teach lessons by passing out numerous written excerpts to be read aloud at specified times. If there are enough excerpts, there may be no time whatever for thinking and discussing. One excellent Sunday School teacher who was obviously very well prepared and knowledgeable about the subject seemed to freeze if anyone suggested a thought or brought up a point she had not previously considered. She would say, "We have to move on now in order to cover our lesson." A teacher is wise, of course, to keep a straight course and avoid asides that do not pertain to the lesson. But if someone raises a question that is relevant to the lesson, it deserves discussion and serious treatment in order to meet the needs of the individual.

It is important for any leader to ask personal questions in an effort to learn the sincere feelings or problems of the person being interviewed. One Relief Society president always began her interviews personally: "How is your family doing? How is your son Kent progressing? Kelly is really growing—how is her testimony? Are you spending enough time with your family?" It always seemed that she had forever to spend in conversation, and so it relaxed the women who served with her and made them more likely to talk candidly and meaningfully. Moreover, they appreciated the personal interest. Here was a leader who successfully transmitted her sincere interest in each person.

I had a similar experience as a missionary in New Zealand many years ago when Spencer W. Kimball toured our mission as an apostle. Before his arrival, I had another interview with a General Authority that had been very brief and to the point: "Is there anything unusual going on in the mission? Are you happy? OK, send in the next one." As a result, I expected something similar with Elder Kimball. Instead, he pulled up his chair close to mine, crossed his legs, and asked many personal questions that required long answers. Even though he had about fifty missionaries to see after me, he never looked at his watch and seemed to concentrate completely on me and my problems. This seemed an excellent example of reaching the one.

Listening with understanding is crucial. It is important for leaders to listen carefully and actively, probing occasionally in order to learn as much as possible, but being careful not to render judgments before understanding all the facts. Often an interview is more successful if the person being interviewed does most of the talking. If the interviewer seems quiet but sincere and engaged, it is a positive sign. Empathetic listening will allow the interviewer to put himself in the shoes of the person being interviewed, to try to understand where he is coming from.

Many leaders make a mistake by asking, "How can I help?" when the person seeking help is often unsure of the answer. Maybe they just need to get something off their chest. Maybe the leader needs to take the initiative by actually *doing* something. He can suggest action such as, "Why don't I visit your quorum next week and observe the problem?" or "I'll be glad to sit down with you and your counselor and help the two of you resolve the problem." How many of us have volunteered to help someone in need with this familiar nonaction: "If you ever need anything, don't hesitate to call on me." And of course, none of us ever do. Instead of being helpful, this stereotyped statement suggests apathy, someone who really does not want to help. It may even be interpreted by the one in need as a challenge to do it alone. Undoubtedly, most people who offer to help others are sincere, but sincerity must be proved by action.

No leader can afford to be afraid of close friendships. Leaders must be with those they lead, not only in formal settings, but "in the trenches." We need to mix with our followers, to get to know them, to understand their problems and concerns. We need to express our interest and love on a sincere, down-to-earth basis, and to be a genuine friend to those we lead.

Chapter Seven

PEOPLE
NOT PROGRAMS

One of the greatest pitfalls for any leader is the desire to develop smooth machinery, impressive statistics and finances, and a favorable image, while the main focus of leadership—people—is neglected. Paul said: "Pure religion and undefiled before God and the Father is this, To visit the fatherless and widows in their affliction, and to keep himself unspotted from the world." (James 1:27.) It is important to remember that no matter how well oiled the machinery, the program will still fail if it does not reach people and relate to them.

There is no greater opportunity for being close to people than being a parent. At all costs we should avoid the tendency to govern our homes as if they were small bureaucracies where decisions are made on a mechanical basis. We need to spend as much time as possible with our children, no matter what our professional obligations may be. Euphemisms such as "quality time" sometimes trap us into believing that we are doing right by our children when we are not. Cartoonist Garry Trudeau expressed it effectively in one of his "Doonesbury" comic strips: Mark, a talk-show host, was interviewing an author of a book who had included one chapter called "Quality Time." Mark asked him to explain that concept. The author said, "For sure, Mark. Quality time is the kind of time you spend with your kids if you're really too pressed to give them the more traditional quantity time! By giving a child quality time, that is, highly concentrated dosages of focused attention, the busy parent can shave valuable hours off the time required to impact his child's development." Mark replies, "So quality time is basically a time-saver," to which the author responds, "Right. It works with old people, too, by the way."

Some of the most productive times I have had with our children are those one-on-one sessions that are not programmed. Recently, I took a five-mile hike with my son David, who needed to complete a Scouting merit badge. We had an exceptional opportunity to talk about many things that we never would have considered had we not been alone together for that long period of time. Similarly, our family has enjoyed long periods together during our camping trips. On our last trip, the older teenagers elected to take part in other activities, so we were left alone with the three younger boys. In Harold Parker State Forest in Massachusetts, we were faced with a fierce, pelting rainstorm during the night, which caused our tent to spring several leaks. We were greatly relieved that the next two days were sunny and dry, but the forced time together in the tent during the storm enabled us to interact in unexpected, fruitful ways. The variety in the weather and activities allowed us to feel closer to our younger children. We made smores by the fire and told mystery stories at night in our sleeping bags. Everyone helped equally in the work of camping, and no one looked forward to its end. Participating in an activity like camping enables your children to see you as you really are, and sometimes you can influence them in this setting more powerfully than in a more formal family home evening.

Jesus remains the ultimate example. No matter what pressures bore down on him, he always had time for people, whether he knew them or not. Bartimaeus, who was blind, was eager for Jesus to bless him before he left Jericho. He sat by the wayside, and when Jesus passed by he cried out in a loud voice, saying, "Jesus, thou son of David, have mercy on me." Some people tried to silence this man, but he just cried out even more loudly. Jesus asked that the man be brought to him, and said, "What wilt thou that I shall do unto thee?" Bartimaeus answered: "Lord, that I may receive my sight." Then Jesus gave a simple blessing, saying, "Receive thy sight: thy faith hath saved thee." The grateful man was miraculously healed. (Luke 18:35-43.)

In Capernaum, Jesus was teaching inside a house to a large crowd of people. A group of four people came carrying a man who was afflicted with palsy. He was helpless, unable to speak. His friends wanted to bring him to Jesus, but there were so many people that it seemed impossible. They refused to give up. Somehow, they carried the man to the flat roof of the house, and broke part of the roof away, making an opening large enough to lower the palsied man on a couch into the room where Jesus taught. Instead of being angry at this innovative act, which could have been interpreted as arrogance, Jesus was impressed with their determination. Looking compassionately on the man, Jesus said, "Son, thy sins be forgiven thee." Then he added, "Arise, and take up thy bed, and go thy way into thine house." The man arose from the couch and was fully restored to health and walked out, to the amazement of the crowd. (Mark 2:1-13.)

Jesus was supremely interested in the individual. To the woman brought before him accused of adultery, he said, "Neither do I condemn thee: go, and sin no more." (John 8:11.) To Peter who protested, "Depart from me for I am a sinful man, O Lord," he replied, "Follow me and I will make you a fisher of men." (Matthew 4:19.) When Mary, needing mercy and forgiveness, "wasted money with expensive ointment," Jesus would not let them upbraid her because he saw the motive of love. "Let her alone," he said. When his disciples fell asleep and could not watch with him, he said, "The spirit indeed is willing, but the flesh is weak." (Matthew 26:41.) When a young man was not earnest enough to follow him, he expressed his appreciation and compassion, "Then Jesus beholding him loved him."

(Mark 10:21, 22.) Even though this young man was not strong enough to sell all that he had and give it to the poor and follow the Lord, Christ loved him.

Jesus was not quick to judge, but always showed mercy and compassion. He exhibited the desire to practice the spirit of the law above the letter of the law. So Jesus performed mighty miracles: "healing the sick, raising the dead, causing the lame to walk, and the blind to receive their sight, and the deaf to hear, and curing all manner of diseases," and he did some of it on the Sabbath day. (Mosiah 3:5.) Finally, he spent countless hours teaching the gospel to all who would hear. Through parables he taught that man was greater than all his sins.

Joseph Smith once said: "All the religious world is boasting of righteousness: it is the doctrine of the devil to retard the human mind, and hinder our progress, by filling us with self-righteousness. The nearer we get to our heavenly Father, the more we are disposed to look with compassion on perishing souls; we feel that we want to take them upon our shoulders, and cast their sins behind our backs. My talk is intended for all this society; if you would have God have mercy on you, have mercy on one another."[1]

The effective leader will follow the example set by the Master, and will pay the closest attention to people and their needs. Sometimes a parent can be most effective during family nights if he is willing to be unstructured and respond to the needs expressed by his children. During one of our family nights, the subject was anger, and each of us interacted with another member of the family by playing roles illustrating that emotion. It was very much like a series of one-act plays. Then we talked about the meaning behind the words and actions. The children became so involved that they wanted to continue after Marti and I thought it was over, so we improvised and did some other role-playing because it seemed to be an activity that they would remember.

On another evening we had a successful treasure hunt

that taught a gospel theme. Being flexible in family home evenings can be very helpful for parents in meeting specific needs. Sometimes subjects will be brought up for discussion that may at first seem to be diversions from the real purpose of the lesson, when in fact they are an opportunity for meaningful discussion. A "lesson" can come out of objections raised by children to family policies, requests for rule changes, and questions that need clarification.

Parents should constantly look for the "teaching moment" that will allow them and their children to draw closer. It is then that a concept might be taught more effectively than in any structured environment. Recently, I spent a good part of an evening helping my son David prepare for a history exam. At first it seemed the kind of tedious process we had been through many times before, but surprisingly it blossomed instead into a very productive, even stimulating, discussion of history: how it pertains to life and of study techniques. We both enjoyed it, and I had the feeling that David had learned some crucial principles, perhaps more important than the material designed for the exam. Parents need to be sensitive enough to look beyond program and structure to the personalities and needs of their children.

I also believe that interviews with our children are often more rewarding when they occur in unstructured settings, and are not billed in a formal sense as interviews. Driving in the car, eating ice cream or pizza, or even playing basketball together can bring opportunities for deep conversation. I have learned more about my children in these circumstances than when I have just tried to sit down and talk. Many bishops have experienced the same positive results by approaching young people of their wards in unexpected, casual settings. Profound thoughts and more openly expressed opinions are frequently expressed when the pressure to perform is removed.

One new bishop was at first overcome by what seemed like a mountain of detail to master and a list of responsibilities to fulfill. He seemed to be expending his energy in many different directions and getting very little accomplished. Then he decided to concentrate mostly on counseling people of all ages who needed him. He relaxed considerably and felt that although there was much that was undone and much that was delegated to others, he was doing what was most important. He visited the sick and the elderly, and he felt a reassurance that these were the weightier matters of the law.

We once had a road-show director who was dedicated but inexperienced. Initially, we all feared that the final product would be a disaster because the director was simply not equipped to lead it. But she worked very hard to learn, she willingly took a flood of well-meaning suggestions, and she made friends with everyone in the production. She not only earned their respect, but she got to know each person. In the end, the cast loved her. Through the process, she was able to plant a spirit of determination to produce the best possible show that was balanced with a desire to enjoy the experience. We worked hard, but we relaxed a little about the future, convinced that she was a trustworthy leader.

Clearly, leaders should avoid bureaucratic techniques, which usually result in a fixed routine and an assembly-line style. Bureaucracy tends to be efficient because it dehumanizes production, eliminating human error. In any organization dedicated to human needs, the growth of bureaucracy can be unfortunate because those needs may be disregarded in the scramble to turn out a product. Bureaucracy often finds administrators or leaders worried so much about complex procedures, programs, and paper that they forget about human needs. A key to a bureaucracy's competence is its compartmentalization. Each compartment is competent only for its particular expertise, and thus people are often referred from one compartment to another to seek resolution to their problems. Above all, bureaucrats insist on proper procedure. Procedures tend to exclude those served by the bureaucracy from the decision making. Thus, procedures become standard and human needs become less important.[2]

Alexis de Tocqueville, the nineteenth-century French scholar, warned of "an immense and tutelary power" that extended its arm everywhere, covering "the surface of society with a network of small complicated rules, minute and uniform, through which the more original minds and the most energetic characters cannot penetrate, to rise above the crowd."[3]

Hugh Nibley echoed this theme in a brilliant Brigham Young University commencement address entitled "Leadership vs. Management." He noted that no one ever managed men into battle: "Leaders are movers and shakers, original, inventive, unpredictable, imaginative, full of surprises that discomfit the enemy in war and the main office in peace. Managers, on the other hand, are safe, conservative, predictable, conforming organizational men and team players, dedicated to the establishment. . . . Where would management be without the inflexible paper processing, dress standards, attention to proper social, political, and religious affiliation, vigilant watch over habits and attitudes, etc., that gratify the stockholders and satisfy security?

"'If you love me,' said the greatest of all leaders, 'you will keep my commandments.' 'If you know what is good for you,' says the manager, 'you will keep my commandments—and not make waves.' That is why the rise of management always marks the decline of culture."[4]

According to Dr. Nibley, management "feeds on mediocrity," while "leadership is escape from mediocrity." Brigham Young said, "There is too much of a sameness among our people. . . . I do not like stereotyped Mormons—away with stereotyped Mormons!"[5] Dr. Nibley also noted that Jesus chided the Scribes and Pharisees for their one-sidedness: "They kept careful accounts of the most trivial sums brought into the Temple; but in their dealings they neglected fair play, compassion and good faith, which happen to be prime qualities of leadership. The Lord insisted that *both* states of mind are necessary, and that is important: 'These ought ye to have done [speaking of the bookkeeping], and not to leave the other undone.' But it is the blind leading the blind, who reverse priorities, who 'strain at a gnat and swallow a camel.' (Matthew 23:23-24.)"[6]

It seems vital, then, for every leader to protect his own individuality and to utilize original ideas. Even a cursory look at Church history reveals undeniable and impressive diversity among the prophets from Joseph Smith to the present. Brigham Young's practical leadership differed markedly from Joseph Smith's more spiritual style. The kindly, down-to-earth style of George Albert Smith contrasted sharply with the businesslike, disciplined demeanor of Heber J. Grant. More recently, the businesslike, organized administration of Harold B. Lee presented a noticeable contrast to the more gentle qualities of Spencer W. Kimball. Through all those leaders in different generations, the Church prospered. Each prophet brought his own innate talents, interests, and personality to bear on his responsibilities in the Church. Undoubtedly, some people of each generation identified more closely with one leader than another. Because of our own personal qualities, each of us has a favorite style that may fit some leaders and not others, but that does not necessarily mean that any of them are wrong, or ineffective. They are merely individuals with strong, identifiable personalities.

Joseph Smith stressed doctrine and spirituality in the important formative stages of the Church, while Brigham Young lead the Mormon pioneers across the plains with an expertise that was invaluable for that period. He knew how to organize people in such a way as to effectively care for each other's needs and save lives under enormous physical pressures and dangers. Joseph Smith, on the other hand, had provided the charismatic and spiritual strength necessary to inspire people to trust in the Lord.

In a later generation, Heber J. Grant applied his practi-

cal knowledge of financial management to the needs of the
Church in the 20th century during a period of significant
growth. Afterward, George Albert Smith renewed the
spiritual qualities, stressing everyday Christian living with
his own admirable creed as a guide. "I would be a friend to
the friendless and find joy in ministering to the needs of the
poor. . . . I would not seek to force people to live up to my
ideals, but rather love them into doing the thing that is
right."[7]

A similar principle exists in local Church leadership.
One bishop I remember fondly was noted for his down-to-
earth qualities. He had an easy-going, people-oriented demeanor. He was succeeded by a much more organized
man, who gave more interesting talks, and who caused the
ward to function more efficiently than it ever had before.
Immediately after our marriage, Marti and I lived in a ward
presided over by a hard-driving, dedicated bishop who
was determined to achieve one hundred percent home
teaching. He kept a tight rein and considered statistics a
very important gauge of success. He was succeeded by a
man with the opposite philosophy, who showed he believed that people counted more than programs, who stressed quality over quantity, and the attitude and personality
of the ward changed drastically.

I observed closely two contrasting Relief Society presidents. The first was an energetic, gregarious person whose
ultimate strength seemed to be her unusual ability to understand people and relate to them. She was succeeded by
a woman who was resolute, serious, and conscious of detail. She upgraded the programs of the Relief Society, im-
proved teaching, and utilized almost all of the diversified
talents of the group. She emphasized visiting teaching and
percentages went dramatically upward. Each president
was effective in her own way, and each made a unique contribution to the ward.

In any ward or stake where change of leadership occurs, much can be gained. Because leadership is dynamic,

not static, the person who holds a position creates an atmosphere reflecting his views. As Lowell Bennion once said to me, "Change is good—even when it's bad." We can benefit from each personality, emphasis, and style. The result is more likely to be leadership and not management.

Effective leaders will get to know their followers. The Savior said, "I am the good shepherd, and know my sheep." (John 10:14.) All leaders owe it to the people they serve to understand their needs. Some leaders may become so enmeshed in a programmed, mechanical approach that they do not know faces or the names that go with them. If the shepherd knows the flock, he will be more likely to make decisions that are individually based rather than programmed.

I once knew a leader who thought in terms of numbers of people, programs, and handbooks. If a decision was made, she invariably did it "by the book." Because she was wedded to a "system," she rarely remembered the names of the people she served. If she had an interview with someone in which a personal problem was discussed, she seemed to forget the person as soon as the interview was completed. She never made it a practice to follow up on the person's problem with a phone call or succeeding interview. The interview was just plugged into a schedule, and she gave advice based on similar situations she had experienced. She hesitated to deviate from this approach because she wanted to do only those things that were acceptable to her own leaders.

Leaders with this kind of approach rarely retain the confidence of their followers. People who have sought advice from someone expect confidentiality in their problem, but not amnesia. A leader who calls and asks about the progress of the problem, volunteers additional information or ideas garnered since their meeting, and asks if another session would be helpful generates warmth, genuine interest, and friendship.

I had such an experience when I was a college student. I

approached a leader I respected greatly and asked for his advice about a personal problem. We talked, and he offered some advice that seemed sincere. I found it disturbing, however, that he never once asked me what happened after our conversation, how I was doing, or if I needed to talk again. I lost respect for him as a leader and became convinced that he was not really interested in me. It seemed that he was only going through the motions and forgot about me as soon as I left his office. True leadership requires an understanding and interest in the human dimension. It means that mechanical or bureaucratic models may have to be altered from time to time to meet the needs of people.

To be effective with people, leaders need to listen and to react honestly and sensitively. In any setting, leaders are criticized by followers, not always fairly but usually sincerely. Leaders have to be realistic enough about their roles and abilities to be able to accept that criticism. Even if criticisms and suggestions made are not valid, leaders who listen and stay abreast of problems will become more effective. Much criticism is given to leaders only indirectly. It may be that a leader hears rumors or unattributed statements of criticism that may seem cutting or counterproductive. It is silly to ignore such statements, for the presence of criticism itself may suggest need for action, or at least introspection. On the other hand, it is important not to overreact to criticism. Any criticism gives a leader a chance to evaluate his own performance, nonetheless, and to change or adjust if necessary to become more effective, more humane, or more sensitive.

Some people, of course, can become so sensitive to criticism that they lose their ability to lead and sink into mental depression. Usually, not even the critic wants that to happen. It is important for leaders to try to maintain balance between the criticism and their own perception of their performance.

When children criticize parents, those criticisms can be

devastating, but all of us need to be loose enough about that reality to accept those that are legitimately deserved and deal calmly with those that are not. When I first started to cook on a regular basis at our house, I was proud enough of myself that I took unkindly to criticism. Our children were candid in their criticism of my cooking, and I had to grow in my ability to respond rationally to it. Finally, I concluded that my self-image did not rest on my cooking ability even though I wanted to keep improving it.

Recently, when Marti was gone for a weekend, I was cooking a roast chicken for Sunday dinner. Everything came out reasonably well except the gravy, which turned out to be greasy and lumpy. When I realized it, I extended my efforts to try to fix it, but to no avail. All the children had much to say about the quality of the gravy, and instead of crawling into a shell, I just joined in the criticism. I teasingly made a threat that all of them would be grounded if any of them revealed to their mother just how bad the gravy was. When we did the dishes, Charlie rescued the gravy, carefully covered it, and put it in the refrigerator to make sure that his mom would be able to inspect it when she returned home. But after everyone had left the kitchen, I snatched the gravy and destroyed it. After Marti returned we all had a good laugh as the children all dredged up varying descriptions of my alleged domestic skills.

During my tenure as bishop, it seemed that criticism ran in waves. If I was able to keep my morale up, invariably there would be heartening, encouraging, positive experiences to follow. One day I recorded in my journal that "criticism is a very pervasive part of being a bishop." Then I detailed several events occurring on a certain Sunday, between the hours of 6:30 A.M. and 5:00 P.M. We were in the middle of construction for an additional wing of our building, resulting in the disruption of classes. Dirt from the new, unfinished wing was being tracked into the old wing. Young children kept exploring the new wing, then came back to the finished building bringing dirt and rubble. The loss of a wall also produced a colder building. Because of these disruptions, members of the Primary presidency were distressed and criticized me for failing to cancel meetings for that day. In my effort to maintain balance, I reminded them that some people had no buildings at all to meet in, and that the Mormon pioneers often had open air meetings.

Afterward, I sat down with a priesthood leader who had incurred my anger by complaining to a visiting General Authority about one ward program. I thought that he should have mentioned his displeasure first to me. Then one of my counselors informed me that he was moving to California, and therefore, two major projects that he was supervising would be left in jeopardy. Finally, I had a regular interview with the stake president during which he recounted some criticism that had been leveled at me through him. I was immediately angry that these people had not come to me personally. In my journal I called the day "Unbelievable—a very depressing day to be serving as a bishop."

On the other hand, the same journal records another interview with the stake president during which he characterized the two of us as "kindred spirits," complimented me for my work, and said that many people had told him of their love for me. After the revelation on blacks and the priesthood, I had the opportunity to ordain the first black in the history of the Hingham Ward, a singularly uplifting experience. I also had feelings of discernment about some specific problems relating to people in the ward that resulted in positive, optimistic sessions with them. I felt especially grateful for the calling of bishop and was buoyed up by my experiences.

Ongoing criticism is part of the leader's normal work load, and he should examine it honestly, being careful to see it in perspective. Selected critics should not be allowed to represent the entire contribution of any leader. It is axiomatic that good experiences follow bad ones.

Just as leaders must not let criticism get them down, they shouldn't expect too much from their meetings with members who need to discuss their problems and feelings. These meetings can be extremely satisfying, with the leader feeling that he has truly helped. But this isn't always the case. Susan Hainsworth cautioned in an *Ensign* article that "many of us, in our well-meaning efforts to serve, try to take too much responsibility for the lives of others. We feel that we must solve all of the problems that bring sorrow to the people around us. This feeling often leads to anxiety over circumstances we cannot control or to trying to push another person into a solution that she has not chosen."[8]

Even if we cannot exert the kind of influence we would hope for, we can give effective interaction, discernment, and advice. If interviews and counseling sessions are approached prayerfully and sensitively, they will usually be helpful to both parties. There are some people with serious problems who need a listening ear and who may go away from these sessions at least temporarily encouraged. There are people who need someone in an emergency and who are grateful beyond measure for some advice. Jesus said, "Inasmuch as ye have done it unto one of the least of these my brethren, ye have done it unto me." (Matthew 25:40.)

Chapter Eight

HOLDING
EFFECTIVE MEETINGS

Meetings are one of the most important vehicles for carrying out principles of leadership, because they give leaders an opportunity to provide information, set a tone, and inspire followers to greater dedication and service. If handled in inappropriate ways, however, meetings can cause followers to be less inclined to follow the leader's directions.

Throughout time, and certainly through the history of the Church, meetings have been occasionally resented and rebelled against. Elder H. W. Naisbitt gave an address to the old Salt Lake City Thirteenth Ward in 1879 in which he tried to persuade the congregation to realize the importance of attending meetings: "I recollect a person saying to me once, 'Well, who preached today?' 'O brother so and so.' 'Well, I know all he can say; and besides when such and such persons preach I can stay at home and read the Bible and not much of that I think—I can read the Book of Mormon, Doctrine and Covenants, Deseret News, and any of the books published by the Church and I enjoy myself better than I do in going to meeting.' Now is that a fact? A man may think so; but is it a fact that a man can increase in the knowledge of the things of God if he absents himself from the services of the sanctuary as established by divine appointment? I say, no. The meeting house is the place where the table is spread, where the food is prepared by the eternal spirit, and when we go there and hear men speak to us under the influence of that spirit, and we are in possession of the same spirit—we are fed, we grow and increase, and the roots and fibres of our being run deeper, and so enable us to 'bring forth more fruit.'"[1]

Brigham Young used an interesting, direct approach to the same topic: "Let the people come to meeting, and hear what is said, and if any of you are not instructed to your satisfaction, be so kind as to send up a card to the stand, intimating your desire to speak, and we will give you an opportunity of doing so, to display your wisdom; for we wish to learn wisdom and get understanding."[2]

According to Brigham, "One thing is certain, that where people make a practice of attending meetings frequently, it creates an increased desire to do so." He said that even before he was "religious" he enjoyed attending meetings: "For I was anxious to learn; having a thirst for knowledge, I was always gratified in attending meetings to listen to public addresses, to gain instruction and add to my stock of information."[3]

Modern Church leaders have faced the same problem, as evidenced by Matthew Cowley's admonitions. Elder Cowley remembered a great lawyer and patriarch from Idaho who missed the meetings of the high council. "I used to get tired after a long day in court or a long day at the office, and I would go home worn out and weary. I would have a bite to eat, and I would go to a high council meeting or some other meeting, and the burden was just lifted off my shoulders." He said, "I have never had such relaxation or rest in the hard labors of the day as I used to have when I belonged to the high council and went to those meetings."

And yet, said Elder Cowley, "most of us go home tired and miserable and say 'Why do they have so many meetings?' We are always complaining about the meetings. If anyone should complain, I should. Don't worry about these meetings. Go to them. Go to them with the right spirit, and you will have rest."[4]

Elder Cowley was also capable of discussing the issue in a lighter vein: "I have heard some people say, 'Well, it is a day of rest. I can rest better in the movies than I can in Church.' Brothers and sisters, that simply isn't true. I have never seen such beautiful resting, relaxation, in all my life as when I sit in the services of this Church. Ordinarily you don't sleep in movies. I have never seen anybody go to sleep in a ball game, but my, in Church! I don't see why people say in this Church, 'Oh, I am too tired tonight to go to Church. I am too tired. I am going to stay home and rest.'

"One thing I like about the natives down in the islands, is that they never say, 'Oh, I am too tired to go to Church tonight.' Do you know what they say? 'Go to Church and have a good sleep,' and that is just what they do. It is very unusual. They can hear just as well when they are asleep and snoring as they can when they are wide-awake. It doesn't disturb me when people go to sleep in the congregation now because I think of those people down there. I've seen lots of them sound asleep in Church and after meeting come up and tell me about what I told them. It's wonderful to have that gift. I wish I had it."[5]

Leaders should consider that if people fall asleep in meetings or hesitate to attend them, the meetings may need improvement. President Spencer W. Kimball suggested as much when he advised stake presidents and bishops to "take a particular interest in improving the quality of teaching in the Church."

Then he continued: "The Savior has told us to feed his sheep. (See John 21:15-17.) I fear that all too often many of our members come to church, sit through a class or meeting, and they then return home having been largely uninformed. It is especially unfortunate when this happens at a time when they may be entering a period of stress, temptation, or crisis. We all need to be touched and nurtured by the Spirit, and effective teaching is one of the most important ways this can happen. We often do vigorous enlistment work to get members to come to Church but then do not adequately watch over what they receive when they do come."[6]

In speaking about the importance of interesting meetings, Ruth Hardy Funk, former Young Women's general president, recalled the women's conference in which Dwan Young, Ardeth Kapp, and Barbara Winder had spoken. "I have never known in my lifetime when women talked so persuasively from the scriptures. They talked as authorities. They taught the gospel of Jesus Christ. They didn't talk about peripheral matters. It thrilled me more than I can possibly describe."[7]

In any meeting the leader sets the tone, whether it is spiritual, personable, and compassionate; or whether it is distant, dictatorial, awkwardly organized, and dull. People who attend meetings almost immediately sense the nature of leadership in a meeting. A leader, therefore, needs to be confident without being egocentric, cheerful without being flippant, reverent without being too solemn. No matter where the meeting is held or how many people are there, those in attendance can feel the tone of humility. My sister, Mary Lythgoe Bradford, once said that her ideal church meeting would be one held in the round, without podiums or platforms, where no one was above anyone else, and where everyone looked into each other's eyes. Whether such a meeting takes place physically or not, that tone or atmosphere is one that every leader should emulate.

It is vital that every church meeting have a spiritual base. If it is a sacrament meeting with a theme, those asked to speak can provide that framework. The music contributes significantly to the tone and inspires both the speakers and the listeners. If it is a leadership meeting, a leader can offer a spiritual thought that will take little time but set an important tone. There is a greater need to cultivate spirituality in administrative meetings, because they are often more technically oriented.

Leaders who persist in whispering to each other during the meetings about planning details detract from reverence and indicate to their followers that they are largely unprepared. An appropriate spirit can be maintained without resorting to joking and laughing with each other beyond the listening range of the congregation.

All meetings should have prepared agendas that are followed, keeping the leaders organized, keeping vital material from being omitted, and causing the meetings to move faster. If agendas are adhered to, meetings will usually start and end on time, a must in order to inspire confidence. If people are convinced that meetings will end when leaders indicate, they will be more likely to come again.

My most instructive personal experience occurred in a ward in Cambridge, Massachusetts, where I was assigned as a high council speaker. Also in attendance that day was an Idaho bishop who had recently been involved in a flood disaster. The Cambridge bishop asked this visiting bishop to speak briefly prior to my talk and give the congregation the flavor of the crisis. Predictably, he got caught up in the story and continued speaking until the meeting reached its normal ending time. I glanced at the bishop, who leaned over to reassure me, saying, "Take as much time as you like!" I knew immediately what I would do. Standing at the pulpit and observing the nervous fidgeting in front of me, I spoke two simple sentences in which I expressed thanks for the visiting bishop's remarks and hoped that I would have another opportunity to speak to them. Then I sat down. I have never had such an overwhelmingly positive reaction to a talk as I did that day. People were effusive in their praise.

Elder J. Golden Kimball once said: "I remember that not many conferences ago I was called to the stand just before the conference adjourned. President Grant told me I had seven minutes—I took three—and I think it is the only time that President Grant ever shook hands with me after one of my talks. President Grant did not shake hands with me because of what I said; it was because I left him four minutes, and that is more than any of the other brethren have ever done."[8]

On another occasion, he said, "I understand what time means. At the conference six months ago I was fortunate in being called upon, and I occupied three minutes. To my surprise I was complimented everywhere I went. People say it was the best sermon I ever preached."[9]

Many times leaders face changes that endanger the value of a meeting: the people who were to play a leading role cannot be there, the issues that were to be discussed have been resolved, or most of the people invited are out of town. A meeting simply for the sake of meeting is a disservice that causes people to question the wisdom of their leaders. If a meeting is scheduled to be held for purely informational purposes, without need for discussion, or there are just too few issues to warrant it, a cancellation and a memo in the mail will produce heartfelt gratitude from those expected to attend.

In order to generate the most support from followers, meetings should be held at the times that are most reasonable and convenient to the most people involved. It is counterproductive to insist that people travel great distances if there are more desirable alternatives. Leaders should exercise care to schedule meetings at times that would not inconvenience families and limit their time together. It is also wise to exercise compassion toward people who have occasional problems in attendance.

If some people fail to attend meetings regularly, it is better to talk it over individually rather than addressing the issue in front of the entire group. Criticizing the group because some or many do not attend regularly merely weakens confidence in the leaders. It makes it appear to the entire group that many people do not support their leaders or perhaps that they consider the meetings unnecessary. Some of those listening may well reevaluate their own attitudes.

It is usually much more productive for a leader to speak positively about the value of the meeting, illustrating with examples and compliments that were offered, rather than chastising those who were not there. Chastisement in a group setting usually confirms in those who were absent the wisdom of their original choice.

In regularly held meetings, especially leadership meetings, it is vital that those who attend believe that their contributions and comments count and are seriously considered. If they sense that they are called together merely to be instructed or lectured to, with no opportunity to give advice or consent, they may be inclined either to rebellion or apathy.

It is a challenge for any leader to guide a meeting in an organized fashion. It should be designed to start on time and end on time on the one hand, yet be sensitive to the needs and wishes of those in attendance on the other. It is possible to err significantly on either side. I remember a counselor in a stake presidency who desired to run a tight ship and address the agenda expeditiously. We all admired him for that, but unfailingly, whenever anyone described a problem that needed attention, he would say, "I'm sorry, but we have to move on now." We all suffered frustration because no problem ever seemed worthy of extended consideration. The desire to end a meeting should not prevent problems from being resolved.

It should also be noted, however, that if a leader is too flexible with discussion, there may be opportunities to talk well into the night. Another stake presidency member tended toward the free-wheeling approach. When all the business was covered, he would persist in asking several times, "Are you sure there is not anything else that we should consider before this meeting ends?" After the question had been asked twice with appropriate pauses, someone would always introduce a controversial or sensitive topic that was impossible to resolve at such a late hour, but would guarantee the extension of the meeting for another hour. It is possible to have an agenda that provides people with equitable opportunities to present their views. There are some issues that are better resolved in a smaller group,

such as a committee to do research; and there are some issues that are better discussed one-on-one either because
they concern people's confidential problems or because
they do not concern the entire group.

Every leader should be as personal as possible. When
speakers are introduced in sacrament meeting, a leader
should briefly summarize their background so that they
feel appreciated, and the congregation has adequate
knowledge about them. If people are sustained or released
from callings, it is wise to express thanks and praise for
dedication and effectiveness in the position. Leaders who
approach people after meetings and compliment them for
their participation or the expertise they demonstrated in a
calling will be well rewarded. Mingling with members after
the meeting is another relevant sign of the personal approach.

I have always thought it was counterproductive to
"pull a coattail." Everyone has been in meetings where the
speaker exceeded good judgment either in content or
length, and where more than one person would have preferred pulling a coattail, indicating that it was time to sit
down. In one ward, an elderly man who had been devoted
to right-wing political causes most of his life was speaking.
He became much too political for most tastes, and made the
ward leaders very uncomfortable. He also exceeded his
time limit. Finally, without warning, a counselor, who was
conducting, jumped up and literally pulled the man's coattail. Clearly ruffled, the man stopped short, added a few
quick sentences, and then sat down. After the meeting, he
unleashed his embarrassment and fury on the entire
bishopric.

Most people in the congregation were very familiar
with this man. And though most did not share his views,
they recognized his fine, human qualities, respected his life
and example, and could forgive him some of his political
excesses. In short, he was loved and appreciated in spite of
those excesses and most people were not adamant about

whether he should express them in church or not. As a result, it may have been better to sit down with him after the meeting, or prior to his next speaking engagement, and gently outline those items that he should refrain from discussing. In so doing, his feelings and the integrity of the meeting could have been protected without embarrassment for anyone.

The meetings with which we are most familiar is the family home evening, a time when we have a chance to exercise leadership with our families. All the same principles exist in that setting as in a larger, more formal meeting. There should be organization in planning the meeting, with a person to conduct, give the lesson, and call on people to pray. It should start and end on time, and there should be ample opportunity for all members of the family to comment and express their views. In our family, we have found great success in alternating all those responsibilities: conducting, giving the lesson, choosing the music, and planning the games afterward. This gives everyone in the family opportunities to develop principles of leadership.

Sometimes we make a mistake by taking some of the events in a family home evening too seriously. Since it is a smaller group setting, there is a temptation to make comments or jokes that would not be appropriate in a larger meeting. Some parents make the mistake of lecturing children in anger instead of acknowledging the more relaxed atmosphere. Family members should not be allowed to criticize or embarrass each other, of course, but a touch of good-natured humor will not spoil the spirit of a family home evening, and may even enhance it.

Our family home evenings vary in quality, depending on the mood of the family members, the preparation of the teacher giving the lesson, and the subject matter being considered. Sometimes we have become too loose, but mostly we have been able to strike a balance between the serious, formal atmosphere of a church meeting and the more familiar surroundings of home. Since everyone in the family is accustomed to mixing with each other on an informal basis, a formal meeting held once a week is the exception rather than the rule, so it is expected that there will be a lighter spirit.

Similarly, home teachers and visiting teachers usually have more success if they adapt to a more informal setting for giving their messages and inquiring after the welfare of the family. Home teachers and visiting teachers who sternly lecture and give lengthy lessons usually find that the meeting has degenerated, just as do those home teachers and visiting teachers who persist in making the meeting so informal that no religion at all is included. Some home teachers spend their time talking about a variety of issues that have nothing to do with their purpose in calling, a practice that is opposite of the formal approach and just as counterproductive.

Most importantly, meetings of all kinds should be planned carefully enough to fit the needs of the people involved. The result is likely to be fewer examples of rebellion and a greater dedication to meeting attendance. Meetings should be a means to an end, and not an end in themselves.

Chapter Nine

TEACHING
CORRECT PRINCIPLES

It seems fitting that Jesus Christ, who provides us with the best example of leadership is also considered the master teacher. Lowell L. Bennion, in his fine book *Jesus, The Master Teacher*, says: "Jesus was not a classroom teacher, but an itinerant. He taught on the mount, on the shores of Galilee, in a boat, in the marketplace, in a living room, along the highway, in the temple court—wherever he could. We too are itinerant teachers. Wherever we go, whenever we mingle with human beings—at home, at work, at play, in the neighborhood, at church—whether we will or not, we teach those with whom we interact."[1]

The fact that Jesus was such an unusually gifted teacher undoubtedly contributed to his effectiveness as a leader. Through the incomparable use of images, parables, and proverbs, he made his teachings come to life and mean something to his listeners. His parables are creative works of art, a combination of active imagination and a remarkable ability to explain them to his followers. In telling his stories, Jesus cut out unnecessary detail and made his point in a few pithy verses. Economy of language was one of his greatest strengths.

Jesus' sayings, parables, and stories always stress large concepts with universal application. "It is more blessed to give than to receive." (Acts 20:35.) "Man shall not live by bread alone." (Luke 4:4.) "Blessed are the poor in spirit. Blessed are they which do hunger and thirst after righteousness." (Matthew 5:3, 6.)

He taught principles, which he reduced to the great fundamental of love. "Thou shalt love the Lord thy God with all thy heart, and with all thy soul, and with all my mind. This is the first and great commandment. And the second is like unto it, thou shalt love thy neighbour as thyself. On these two commandments hang all the law and the prophets." (Matthew 22:37-40.)

Joseph Smith said: "I teach my people correct principles and they govern themselves." We should teach correct principles so that our students can think for themselves and govern themselves. Jesus said, "Woe unto you, scribes and Pharisees, hypocrites! for ye pay tithe of mint and anise and cummin [spices], and have omitted the weightier matters of the law, judgment [justice], mercy, and faith: these ought ye to have done, and not to leave the other undone." (Matthew 23:23.)

Jesus concentrated more on the student than on the subject matter. When the scribes and Pharisees brought a woman to him who was accused of adultery, it was evident that they did not care about the woman's feelings. They quoted the law of Moses, which said she should be stoned. Jesus' reply was, "He that is without sin among you, let him first cast a stone at her." Her accusers walked away, one by one. He told the woman to go and sin no more. (John 8:1-11.) It was not that he condoned adultery, but rather his view of chastity was more profound than the law of Moses. This woman needed compassion and mercy, and he considered her greater than the law of Moses. Her accusers also needed a lesson in love.

To be student-centered as a teacher is to be people-centered as a leader. All people cannot be treated alike; some may need to be rebuked while some need compassion. Some may need strong words, while others need a shoulder to cry on. I remember one young woman who was in the process of divorce who sought my advice on a new relationship she had formed with a man. He had suggested that they move in together, and although she knew it was wrong, she was so emotionally overwrought that she thought she needed his support. They intended to get married when they could, so she wondered why it was so wrong to move in together. I felt impelled to advise her against the move and to accept no compromise. Initially, she seemed determined to do it anyway. But when she realized that I was inflexible, she thought it over and thanked me profusely for "saving" her from a great mistake. After the divorce was final, she married the man, he accepted the gospel, and they are building a very happy life together.

On the other hand, another young woman approached me to confess the sin of fornication. She was distraught, humble, and determined to turn her life around. Since I did not have to convince her of the need to change, I tried to give her compassion and love. She needed to understand that there was a way back, and that she could find happiness with the Lord's help.

A teacher's responsibility is to change someone's life for the better. Brooks Adams once said, "A teacher affects eternity; he can never tell where his influence stops."[2] Certain teachers stand out in my memory for influences they had on me at various stages of my life. The most powerful memory is of Sister Glazier, a Sunday School teacher with a very large voice. She was my teacher when I was a very little boy, and she told numerous biblical stories with such flair that I could see the events passing before my eyes. I was fascinated by her teaching and looked forward to it. Except for my own mother, she may have been the single most important teacher in my life, because she influenced me positively at my most formative time. My mother spent long hours with me, one-on-one, teaching me principles and telling stories from the scriptures and from her own experience. For birthdays or other special occasions, we went downtown together to eat and see a movie. Her influence on me was profound and positive.

The two other teachers I remember from my early years

were both deacons quorum advisers. Lyle Johnson was my Scoutmaster and quorum adviser. He obviously loved us and enjoyed being with us, and he encouraged us to call him by his first name. Together we participated in many activities outside of the structured meetings and classes. I especially enjoyed going bowling with him and the deacons quorum. Lyle taught us principles that I can still remember, most notably the structure and efficacy of prayer, how to pray effectively, and what prayer means to us. When he was released, Hal West took his place. He was equally effective, and I continued to love the classes and the interaction with him and the other members of the quorum. Both these teachers gave willingly and enthusiastically of their time for us.

At Olympus High School in Salt Lake City, I remember most vividly Barbara Beal, an English teacher who was interesting, personal, and knowledgeable; who taught me to love literature and language; and Gerald Christensen, a history teacher who unwittingly taught me to love history by giving me a C on a test when I thought I deserved an A. To show him that I was capable of an A, I studied harder than I ever had before, won an A in the class, and developed a continuing love for history.

At the University of Utah, I discovered how exciting learning could be by taking a history course from the inimitable Dr. David E. Miller. Even at 7:45 A.M., Professor Miller was unbelievably enthusiastic, funny, and stimulating. His sense of humor and his extensive knowledge mesmerized me during virtually every class. He did not recite lists or events, but rather taught major themes and then illustrated them with anecdotes and stories. He usually managed to suggest ways that these stories had some relevance to modern life. At the conclusion of the course, I was sure that history should be my college major.

Later, as a graduate student I was equally stimulated by two more professors of exceptional ability, Alfred Cave and James Clayton. Professor Cave spoke enthusiastically without notes and hammered home principles that he explained carefully. He was so obviously dedicated to excellence that he made us want to perform at our best capability. When I presented a paper in his seminar, I worked harder than I ever had in my life. Professor Clayton made me uneasy by using the Socratic method, asking questions that were designed to make us think. I always left the classroom thinking about some new idea that he had presented.

When I became a professor myself, I tried to emulate these teachers when I taught my own students. I combined the methods I admired in them, and added my own style. I had become convinced that no teacher could be successful with students unless he could be *interesting*. I tried to tell stories that would add interest and I made it clear that there was a lesson to be learned from each one. I tried to make history relevant to the present. If I could see an example from today's news that would make an event or theme from yesterday more interesting or important, I would explain both and tie them together.

In some classes I have felt a rapport that would indicate that these methods had achieved some success. In one-on-one counseling sessions I have noticed that individual students can respond sincerely to specific advice. If only one student reacts positively, teaching becomes a uniquely satisfying experience. Many teachers can attest to that fact because of letters they have received later in life from students whose lives were touched.

Jesus also was devoted to making people think. He stimulated them by his style of teaching. He was provocative in the way he asked and answered questions. "For what is a man profited, if he shall gain the whole world, and lose his own soul? or what shall a man give in exchange for his soul?" (Matthew 16:26.) An entire class discussion can ensue from this brief question. Toward the end of his life, Jesus provoked the Twelve into understanding the purpose of his earthly mission by asking this question, 'Whom do men say that I the Son of man am?" After several responses, he asked, "But whom say ye that I am?"

When a lawyer asked Jesus, "Master, what shall I do to inherit eternal life?" Jesus chose not to answer directly, but to ask a question of his own: "What is written in the law? how readest thou?" The lawyer answered and Jesus commended him, and then the lawyer asked, "Who is my neighbour?" Then Jesus told the parable of the Good Samaritan and ended by asking the question, "Which now of these three, thinkest thou, was neighbour unto him that fell among thieves?" The lawyer got the point and replied, "He that shewed mercy on him." Jesus said, "Go, and do thou likewise." (Luke 10:25-37.)

It is important that we teach people to consider the gospel a rational as well as a spiritual entity, and that the restoration process began with the intellectual and spiritual quest of a young man.

Dr. Louis Agassiz, the distinguished naturalist, was approached by an obscure spinster woman in London after he had given a lecture. She complained to him that she had never had a chance in life. She ran a boarding house and Dr. Agassiz asked her what she did.

"I skin potatoes and chop onions," she said.

He said, "Madam, where do you sit during these interesting but homely duties?"

"On the bottom step of the kitchen stairs," was her reply.

"Where do your feet rest?"

"On glazed brick."

"What is glazed brick?"

"I don't know, sir."

He said, "How long have you been sitting there?"

She said, "Fifteen years."

"Madam, here is my personal card. Would you kindly write me a letter concerning the nature of a glazed brick?"

She took this challenge seriously and went home and researched the nature of brick. She found an encyclopedia definition of glazed brick as vitrified kaolin and hydrous aluminum silicate. She was curious as to what that meant, and so she read all she could find about the word *vitrified*.

She did the same with the word *hydrous*. Then she visited museums and brickyards, finding the history of more than 120 bricks and tiles, and why there had to be so many. Finally, she sat down and wrote thirty-six pages on the subject of glazed brick and tile.

Dr. Agassiz's reply said, "Dear Madam, this is the best article I have ever seen on the subject. If you will kindly change the three words marked with asterisks, I will have it published and pay you for it." A little while later, she received another letter and $250. At the bottom of the letter was the query in pencil, "What was under those bricks?" In a single word she replied in her own note, "ants." He wrote back saying, "Tell me about the ants."

This woman next studied ants, finding between eighteen hundred and twenty-five hundred different kinds. There are ants that are very tiny, ants that are an inch long and march in solid armies a half mile wide, ants that are blind, ants that get wings on the afternoon of the day they die, ants that keep cows to milk. The spinster completed her study and then wrote Dr. Agassiz 360 pages on the subject. He published the book and sent her the money, and she went to visit the countries she had dreamed about all her life.[3] Dr. Agassiz used the mark of a great teacher in stimulating this woman to great personal achievement.

Jesus showed us how to take advantage of the teaching moments, those rare opportunities when someone is vulnerable to understanding a principle. He saw rich men casting their gifts into the treasury, and a poor widow casting in two mites. He said to his listeners, "Of a truth I say unto you, that this poor widow hath cast in more than they all." (Luke 21:1-3.) He took the moment at the well to tell the woman: "If thou knewest . . . who it is that saith to thee, Give me to drink; thou wouldest have asked of him, and he would have given thee living water." She did not understand. He continued, "Whosoever drinketh of this water shall thirst again; but whosoever drinketh of the water that I shall give him shall never thirst; but the water

that I shall give him shall be in him a well of water spring-
ing up into everlasting life." (John 4:5-15.)

My sixteen-year-old daughter's Sunday School teacher
was highly successful from the first Sunday he took the
class. That week he telephoned me and requested that I
bring an object or possession of Kelly's to him on Sunday
so that he could use it in commenting about her in class. He
intended a brief biographical sketch of each class member
to convince each of them of his personal interest. A few
weeks later I noticed in the mailbox a letter for Kelly from
her teacher. She said it was a rather long one in which he
asked many questions about her and chatted. I asked why
he would do such a thing, and she said she did not know.
The next day, when another letter came from him, I was
really curious. "What is it this time?" I asked. She said this
one was entirely different—it was just a single question. It
said, "Dear Kelly, what's up? Chet." She decided it must
have something to do with the Sunday School lesson. On
Sunday when he had all the class together, it was evident
that all members of the class had received two letters that
week—one lengthy, chatty one, and one brief one. He
asked the class: "If you were Heavenly Father, how would
you like to receive a prayer like that second letter I sent
you?" This effective, thoughtful teacher had managed to
capture the imaginations of each member of his class for an
entire week, and then cap it off with a relevant lesson on
prayer that all of them will long remember.

If someone asks a question that is obviously sincere, we
should reply to it *now*, even if it takes us slightly off the
track. If someone gives an answer in different words than
we expected, but with the same meaning, we should accept
it as if it were just what we wanted. Never insist on exact
words. Teaching moments come to teachers, to parents,
and to leaders in a variety of situations, inside and outside
a classroom. When mingling with people we should go to
the trouble to make an explanation when we are asked for
one. It is important that the listener be ready to hear the an-

swer, and that the answer be as brief and concise as we can make it.

The scriptures clearly state the obligation of parents to teach their children. They are expected to teach the gospel to their children when they are eight years old, or the sin will be upon their heads. "And they shall also teach their children to pray, and to walk uprightly before the Lord." (D&C 68:25-29.) The scriptures also make it clear that teaching is an obligation that extends to all people.

"And I give unto you a commandment that you shall teach one another the doctrine of the kingdom.

"Teach ye diligently and my grace shall attend you, that you may be instructed more perfectly in theory, in principle, in doctrine, in the law of the gospel, in all things that pertain unto the kingdom of God, that are expedient for you to understand; of things both in heaven and in the earth, and under the earth; things which have been, things which are, things which must shortly come to pass; things which are at home, things which are abroad; the wars and the perplexities of the nations, and the judgments which are on the land; and a knowledge also of countries and of kingdoms—that ye may be prepared in all things." (D&C 88:77-81.)

Clearly, the gospel embraces the importance of learning and teaching under the influence of the Spirit, "and if ye receive not the Spirit ye shall not teach." (D&C 42:14.) No leader should ever underestimate the importance and the power of teaching. All leaders are teachers whether they intend to be or not. The impact generated by purposeful, personal teaching cannot be measured. It is the best opportunity that leaders have to influence individuals.

Chapter Ten

THE ART
OF DELEGATION

Inspiring others to act and to adequately utilize their abilities represents one of the great challenges of any leader. James MacGregor Burns said: "Some define leadership as leaders making followers do what *followers* would not otherwise do, or as leaders making followers do what the *leaders* want them to do; I define leadership as leaders inducing followers to act for certain goals that represent the values and the motivations—the wants and needs, the aspirations and expectations—*of both leaders and followers.* And the genius of leadership lies in the manner in which leaders see and act on their own and their followers' values and motivation."[1]

No matter where the leadership is exercised, it cannot be effective if it is done in a dictatorial manner. The leader must motivate the follower to work for shared goals in a way that meets the needs, wants, and aspirations of both of them. It is not an easy task and any leader invariably asks, "How do I get my work done most effectively?" and "How do I get people to help me?" Those of us who have watched leaders struggle in this way have probably said, "Why doesn't he delegate more?" or "She should learn how to delegate."

People in a variety of leadership roles are prone to failure in delegation. Parents, for instance, often fail to delegate tasks to their children because they do not trust them with an important task. They may also be more interested in getting the job done expeditiously than in investing time

in teaching children responsibility and skills. This is especially understandable where young children are concerned, and yet it is worthwhile to expend the effort.

Young children are often interested in helping with
meal preparations. Realizing this, I have often found myself rushing to finish fixing a meal without the child finding
out, so that I won't have to take the time to let him participate. (Who needs five-year-old Spencer standing on a chair
next to him?) Even if we decide to make the effort, we are
inclined to take from the children the most difficult tasks.
"I'd better break those eggs myself!" or "You're too little to
pour in the flour."

While children may slow down the process, they are
still learning from it. As they get older, they will become
proficient in the kitchen and more self-sufficient when they
need to be. Wise parents who are patient enough to involve
their children in cooking and meal preparation will some
day see the dividends.

My experience with lawn mowing is probably similar to
that of many parents. When my children used to mow the
lawn, they would not get the mower close enough to the
borders. This left long grass around the edges of the yard.
One day, in her effort to follow my instructions, my daughter Kelly accidently broke a basement window. Afterward,
I decided to personally mow the borders before she mowed
the rest of the lawn. As I learned later, this effectively
robbed her of learning to do her best work, as well as feeling entrusted with the full responsibility.

Similarly, as my son reached driving age, I continued to
take the car to the service station for refueling instead of
leaving both the task and the expense to him. Driving a car
entails certain responsibilities that every driver must accept. Taking some of them away, for whatever noble
reason, denies the potential driver the full experience that
pertains to driving. Whether in the home, in church, or in
our workday world, we all experience the temptation to
keep the most important tasks under our control.

Unwillingness or inability to delegate, then, represents a powerful weakness in leadership potential. A leader must never become so enmeshed in detail, that he loses touch with the overall picture. A parent makes a mistake in keeping the lawn as his own private preserve, even if he is convinced that he will do a better job than his children. A bishop should not personally staff and operate the Primary organization, even if he is convinced that he can do a better job than the Primary president. Every leader needs to become converted to the values and benefits of delegation, and then carry it out as effectively as possible.

One of the best offices to exemplify the importance of delegation is the presidency of the United States, purported to be one of the more burdensome offices in the world. Calvin Coolidge, president from 1923-1929, said: "In the discharge of the duties of the office there is one rule of action more important than all others. It consists in never doing anything that someone else can do for you. Like many other good rules, it is proven by its exceptions. But it indicates a course that should be very strictly followed in order to prevent being so entirely devoted to trifling details that there will be little opportunity to give the necessary consideration to policies of large importance."[2]

I served for approximately one year as a bishop without the aid of an executive secretary. It seemed at the time that there were always more important positions crying out for people's service, and so I could justify filling my own calling and that one too. When I finally called an executive secretary, I discovered a massive change in my work schedule. I had been spending an inordinate amount of time on the telephone, arranging for appointments and taking care of details. When the executive secretary suddenly absorbed those duties, and did them very well, I was amazed at how much time I had for other things. It took me some time initially, however, to learn how to effectively use the services of this new person, because I had become so accustomed to doing everything myself. During the transition period, it seemed that I was busier than ever, and finally, a burden was miraculously lifted. Effective delegation provides more time for the leader to spend in other matters of greater importance; but in the short term, he or she may think it takes more time to teach another person the task than to do it personally.

Connie Woolstenhulme, president of the Ricks College Fifth Ward Relief Society, recognized the need to delegate: "If you don't delegate, you would be stuck. If you tried to do everything yourself, you wouldn't get your schoolwork done. Sometimes I wonder if I've neglected Relief Society, particularly in visiting the girls, but it seems to work out in the end if I do the best I can."[3]

Some tasks are easy to delegate, such as assigning a person to give a talk during a scheduled meeting or bring three pounds of ground beef to a Church dinner. Delegating other responsibilities can be more complicated. As a result, many leaders refrain from doing so. What they often do not realize is that the sheer weight of all the responsibilities will catch up with them and weaken their overall performance. They need to conserve strength and effectiveness. No leader can be spread too thin and expect satisfactory results.

It is also possible to have too little concern for detail, and too great a desire to delegate. I once knew a leader who by temperament and training was not a detail person. Even on issues where she was well informed, she chose consciously to focus on broad goals and leave the details to others. She also had a great many other recreation and business interests that required her time and talents. She seemed to see herself as an executive decision-maker, a kind of "chairman of the board" who would oversee a variety of events, but always with comfortable distance.

She delegated so heavily that she lost touch with the meaning and impact of many of the activities she presided over. When someone was disturbed about the way an event turned out, she would refer that person to the chief planner, as if she really carried no responsibility for it. In doing so, she seemed unburdened and carefree, but also remarkably out of touch with many significant problems. When she became aware of problems, she was heavily dependent on the opinions of others to inform her of the necessary details.

Her style was to parcel out mail, responsibilities, and paperwork to a variety of people. Consequently she rarely had any document in her briefcase that would help her act or speak authoritatively on any issue. Once a task was delegated, she trusted the person implicitly, and usually failed to follow through on how the job was progressing. Some people interpreted this technique as impressive confidence, while others feared that she actually did not care about the result. In any case, it was not an example of the most effective type of leadership.

It is important for a leader to be free for the most important responsibilities, making possible the long view and the perspective to be wise. On the other hand, leaders should not delegate so heavily that they actually become incognito, perceived by their followers to be inactive, out of touch, or uninterested in day-to-day considerations.

According to William G. Dyer, there are at least seven steps to effective delegation.[4] The first is to *seek inspiration.* Prayerful consideration will result in a better decision for the leader as well as the person being delegated with the responsibility.

The second is to *give challenging assignments.* There is a common practice among leaders to parcel out only the difficult or boring assignments to other people and keep the interesting ones for themselves. A person who is given a boring assignment will have a difficult time becoming excited about it or dedicated to its completion. If support is really expected, a leader should have enough faith in the person to trust her with some very treasured task.

Sometimes it is difficult for Church leaders in large

wards to provide equally challenging assignments for everyone. Everyone is not like a friend of mine who claims that his fondest hope in the Church is to be called as "second counselor to the magazine representative." I once knew a person in a large ward who had the assignment of being "assistant quiet book director," something she tried to do well, but which left her feeling unfulfilled. A newly baptized member was called to be in charge of our ward building during stake activities. Some people suspected that it was a "nothing" job, but in actuality it seemed to challenge this person effectively as well as fill a genuine need. People coming into the building to hold a dance, for instance, were unfamiliar with the layout of the building, how and where to dispose of garbage, how to operate the sound system, how to find the equipment to clean up, and so forth. This person filled these needs by providing information and guidance, and he did so very effectively. After moving to another state, he was given no Church position in a large ward and has since drifted into inactivity.

On the other hand, I once made the mistake of giving a new member a task that may have been either too challenging or just not suited to his abilities. I asked him to be magazine representative. This required that he keep people informed about their subscriptions to Church magazines and try to inform people who were not subscribers about the advantages of reading them. The job seemed to confuse him very quickly. He submerged into inactivity and has never returned. Although it is difficult to provide the right balance between challenging assignments and room to breathe, it is important to try.

President N. Eldon Tanner said: "Those delegated must be given a meaningful stewardship. Assigning the stewardship is the duty of the leader. Each individual must accept the asigned stewardship and commit himself to perform the duties as he is taught. He must be given the authority as well as the responsibility. Socrates is reported to have said, 'Whatever duty thou assignest me, sooner would I die a thousand times than to forsake it.'"[5]

Sometimes, a leader may think he is testing someone on a smaller, less challenging task. In fact, there may be no opportunity to see him at his best. People do better at the things they *want* to do.

The third step in effective delegation is to *clarify expectations*. In other words, the responsibility should be clearly defined, so that there is no misunderstanding of what the leader would like to see accomplished. Leaders are sometimes guilty of issuing a call to someone, yet failing to outline the specific responsibilities. Even people with exceptional talent may not perform up to expectation if they do not understand what is expected of them.

Sometimes we may be so anxious to drop a certain burden, that we simply throw it at someone and heave a sigh of relief. I'm always telling my five-year-old son to put away his clothes. He tells me he has put them away, but when I go into his room I still see some of them on the floor. When I ask him why, he says, "I'm not tall enough to hang them up." It is really impossible for me to blame him for not being able to accomplish what I have failed to teach him to do. Either I need to do the job for him, or I must spend the time necessary to teach him that he can put away his clothes if he stands on a chair.

We should always take the time to explain a task and make it clear what *we* expect to come from it. An adult may find desirable ways to fill a Church assignment that we never even dreamed of. But we still owe it to that person to let him know what we expect.

Fourth, it is important to *get a commitment*. If the person being given a calling has an opportunity to respond and commit himself to acccomplish it, then there is an agreement to honor. Too often leaders call people to Church positions in a tentative manner: "I realize this will be difficult for you with all your other responsibilities, but if you could just do the best you can." Sometimes a leader will make it possible for the person receiving the call to decline a commitment. "If it doesn't work out, just let me know. Everyone will understand if you can't be _____ and _____.

Don't worry about it." Such an easygoing approach seems the opposite of commitment.

We owe it to the people being given a responsibility to give them the full vision or potential of the job. We should challenge them to utilize every talent. If personal problems result in a need to lessen the commitment, then that can be considered realistically at the appropriate time; but we should not invite anyone to do a job halfheartedly.

Fifth, it is necessary for the leader to *give training as needed.* In fact, Joseph Smith said, "I teach my people correct principles, and they govern themselves." A leader should follow the prophet's example and teach the person called what is needed to function effectively in the position. If there is another leader who is more knowledgeable about this responsibility, then that leader should do it. If someone is asked to be a visiting teacher, for instance, the visiting teaching process should be explained. It should be pointed out that making advance appointments makes for a more productive relationship with visiting teaching families; that prayers and religious messages should be given in the home; and that the visiting teacher should express a sincere interest in the life and activity of the sister and her family, and offer to help in case of emergency or problems. A person who has never been visiting teaching should have an opportunity to observe an experienced woman carry out the assignment. Finally, the person being called should understand that she can utilize the leader for any additional help or advice to assist her in being successful.

As a high councilor, I had occasion to make a call to a new elders quorum president in whom I had great confidence. He accepted the calling unconditionally, and because I was so impressed with his approach and manner, I made the mistake of leaving him on his own. Within a few months it became apparent that in spite of his good intentions, the quorum was not being lead effectively.

The first counselor was making most of the decisions,

not because he was trying to subvert the president's authority but because he was getting no guidance and felt impelled to move the work along. I discovered that the president had not held any presidency meetings, and that he had not assigned any tasks to his counselors. The quorum existed from week to week on inertia. The president was obviously a person of genuine promise who had such little leadership experience that he did not know where to begin. He simply needed training. Belatedly, I began to train him, approaching first such basic matters as scheduling and conducting presidency meetings.

After a task has been delegated, a leader may assume that he can relax and let the person complete it, but leadership requires *follow through*—our sixth step. This need not be done in an obnoxious way, with constant harassment. Rather, the leader should make a regular schedule of consultation, giving the person a chance to report on progress made. At that time, the leader can make further suggestions or clarifications and help to teach the person in his calling. This process will also convince the person that the leader wants to help and is genuinely interested in the outcome.

The seventh point is that the leader must *let go,* allowing the other person the right to do the job consistent with his own skills, personality, style, and experience. It is terribly frustrating to be given a job and then be watched over, regulated, and directed by someone else who feels he must control everything to make sure it is done just as he wants it."[6] The beauty of leadership is that it offers other people the chance to display their individuality and talents. They may be just as dedicated to the task as the leader would be, but the result is entirely different. If a wife expects her husband to share domestic responsibilities in the home, she should not be surprised if his cleaning techniques or cooking skills and tastes are different than hers.

N. Eldon Tanner said, "A leader should never try to do the work of one to whom he has made an assignment. As

President Harold B. Lee said, 'Let them do everything within their power, and you stand in the background and teach them how to do it. I think therein is the secret of growth, to fix responsibility.'"[7]

Usually a task will be completed with more flair and with more dedication if the person is allowed the freedom to display his own personality. Leaders also may have a tendency to hover over the person, causing him to be afraid to act independently, and thus lose individuality and desire. One of the worst mistakes any leader can make is to take over another person's responsibility. One good example of that temptation may be seen in home teaching. One bishop used a heavy hand and a sharp eye to guarantee that home teaching was done. According to his systematic approach, the home teacher was to report by the twentieth of the month on how many families had been home taught. If there were some families not visited by then, it was the bishop's desire that priesthood leaders pick up the slack. They were instructed to go out personally and home teach those people who had not yet been visited. Two or three days later, the bishop himself would call on the homes of the priesthood leaders and ask them the results of home teaching to date. If any homes hadn't been visited, the bishop would encourage them to go immediately. Then, unwilling to wait for these results, the bishop would personally call on all the families not yet home taught.

The result was that a typical person whose home teacher had not come by the twentieth of the month would be individually visited in subsequent days by the elders quorum president, the bishop, and finally the home teacher, all in rapid succession. Some people were offended, because they saw themselves reduced to statistics and their time was being violated with impunity. It could be argued that such a tactic was not home teaching at all, because the home teacher's role was being subverted or taken over by other leaders. Those who "imitated" the home teacher actually detracted from his impact as well as from the faith the people had in their home teachers. They also knew that the home teacher was being chastised in the form of those additional visits by priesthood leaders, and that reduced their respect for their home teacher.

Many parents experience the same temptation with the responsibilities they give their children. Some of us may fear giving our children a certain responsibility because we don't have faith that they will complete it. If we do assign the task, we are tempted to come along afterward and clean it up, clearly showing them that we do not have faith in their ability or determination to carry it out. If my son clips the grass, I may come along afterward and clean up what he misses. If he loads the dishwasher, I may come along afterward and change the distribution of the load, proving to him that I don't like the job he has done. Some parents constantly harass or correct their children while they're trying to accomplish a task, until they feel no desire to complete it. Delegation of a task requires faith in the person entrusted with it.

Praise is also a vital ingredient in the delegation of authority. Even if the job has been done imperfectly, there is usually some facet that we can focus on to express appreciation. Offering deserved compliments and expressing sincere gratitude shores up a person's confidence, increases self-esteem and makes him feel appreciated. Every person needs to know of his leader's positive feelings about the job he is doing. If any leader is to be effective, he has to inspire confidence, love, and trust from those who are asked to follow.

Chapter Eleven

LEADING THROUGH KNOWLEDGE

To lead effectively, leaders must understand principles of leadership as well as the projects for which they have responsibility. Study and learning are imperative for any leader to speak with conviction and to act with knowledge.

The process of education for Church members was exemplified even before the organization of the Church. Joseph Smith went to the Sacred Grove searching, eager to learn, and asking sincere questions. There is no finer symbol of Mormonism than this experience of a young boy seeking God in prayer. His search did not end with the First Vision. He continued to ask questions, to search, and to learn—line upon line, precept upon precept. In this way, modern scripture unfolded through the translation of the Book of Mormon and the revelations that became the bulk of the Doctrine and Covenants. Joseph Smith often prefaced the revelations by saying, "I inquired of the Lord and received the following."

The scriptures themselves are replete with advice to seek learning of all kinds. We should "study and learn, and become acquainted with all good books, and with languages, tongues, and people." (D&C 90:15.) We should diligently seek learning from "the best books . . . even by study and also by faith." (D&C 88:118.) More specifically, the advice given to Joseph Smith was to teach diligently, "that you may be instructed more perfectly in theory, in principle, in doctrine, in the law of the gospel, in all things that pertain unto the kingdom of God, . . . Of things both in heaven and in the earth, and under the earth; things which have been, things which are, things which must shortly come to pass; things which are at home, things which are abroad; the wars and the perplexities of the nations, and the judgments which are on the land; and a knowledge also of countries and of kingdoms—That ye may be prepared in all things. . . . "(D&C 88:78-80.)

An analysis of that passage suggests that the Lord believes that we should be familiar with all disciplines of study—geology, history, contemporary affairs, foreign affairs, war, astronomy, countries, politics,—in fact everything around us. "The glory of God is intelligence, or, in other words, light and truth." (D&C 93:36.)

Hugh B. Brown, former member of the First Presidency, who was especially well-known for his encouragement of learning, said: "I hope that you will develop the questing spirit. Be unafraid of new ideas for they are the steppingstones of progress. You will, of course, respect the opinions of others but be unafraid to dissent—if you are informed.

"Now I have mentioned freedom to express your thoughts, but I caution you that your thoughts and expressions must meet competition in the market place of thought, and in that competition truth will emerge triumphant. Only error needs to fear freedom of expression. Seek truth in all fields, and in that search you will need at least three virtues: courage, zest, and modesty. The ancients put that thought in the form of a prayer. They said, 'From the cowardice that shrinks from new truth, from the laziness that is content with half truth, from the arrogance that thinks it has all the truth—oh God of truth deliver us.'"[1]

On another occasion, President Brown urged his listeners to seek broad learning: "While making a lifetime study of the standard works of the Church, one should also become familiar with the classics, with Shakespeare, Milton, Tennyson, and Wordsworth. He should read something of the philosophers and scientists, should find out how boundaries of knowledge have been altered and extended in religion and in literature. One should know something of the writings of Plato, Aristotle, Socrates, and the late philosophers, who, while they err in many respects, will start a man thinking independently and courageously on the meaning of life and its purpose."[2]

Finally, President Brown made this particularly incisive comment on testimony: "I'm impressed with the testimony of the man who can stand and say he knows the gospel is true, but what I would like to ask is, 'But sir, do you know the gospel?' I say it is one thing to know the gospel is true and another to know what the gospel is. Mere testimony may be gained with but perfunctory knowledge of the Church and its teachings as evidenced by the hundreds who are now coming into the Church with but bare acquaintanceship. But to retain testimony and to be of service in building up the Lord's kingdom requires a serious study of the gospel and knowing of what it is."[3]

Camilla Kimball spent a virtual lifetime taking university classes in English, philosophy, typing, botany, history, public speaking, Bible studies, and literature. She encouraged her children to do the same, and the four of them earned a total of ten college degrees.

She said: "I have always had an inquiring mind. I am not satisfied just to accept things. I like to follow through and study things out. I learned early to put aside those gospel questions that I could not answer. I had a shelf of things I did not understand, but as I have grown older and studied and prayed and thought about each problem, one by one I have been able to understand them better.

"A woman, to be well rounded in her personality, needs many experiences in and out of the home. She needs to be concerned with church, school, and community. If she buries herself inside four walls, she does not reach her potential. She needs to keep growing, to keep aware of the world in which her children are growing. In order to do this, she should be interested in educational advancement and worthwhile endeavors in her community."[4]

Ardeth Kapp has eloquently encouraged scripture study for anyone to acquire necessary gospel learning: "I want to share with you an experience I had this summer. I spent three days in a wilderness camp with 150 youth. We did a lot of hiking and had some hard physical challenges like when we rappelled down an 80 foot cliff. On the last day we were given instructions to go into the woods alone. Before leaving the group, each youth was given a letter from home which had been written by his or her mother or father for this occasion.

"When I went out alone, I took my scriptures with me. I read about my Father in Heaven's love for all of us and for me. It was then that I realized that these scriptures are like letters from home.

"After a time we gathered together. Everyone had opened and read his or her letter. One young woman stood expressing the feelings of her heart. She held her letter close. In her words, 'I nearly bawled my face off when I sat there alone and realized how much my mom and dad love me.' I nearly bawled my face off when I read again about how very much our Father in Heaven loves us.

"Can you imagine being away from home and receiving a letter from your parents and not bothering to open it or read it? This is what happens when we don't read these precious records. The holy scriptures are like letters from home telling us how we can draw near to our Father in Heaven. He tells us to come as we are. No one will be denied. He loves every one."[5]

Carolyn Rasmus, a Brigham Young University professor, echoed that thought: "Sometimes we say, 'If you pray and read the scriptures, you'll have all the answers.' But it's true. We absolutely cannot negate the power and the direction that comes from the scriptures."[6]

Most people expect their leaders to be knowledgeable. As a missionary in New Zealand, I discovered that both current and prospective Church members tended to implicitly trust the word of a missionary. If there was a question to be posed, it was likely that a missionary would be asked to respond. If a missionary made a comment in a Sunday School, it was often interpreted as the "last word." Later, as a bishop, I discovered a similar attitude on the part of ward members. Not only procedural and doctrinal questions, but secular questions were usually brought to the bishop to settle. Some people even expected him to be omniscient.

A well-informed leader commands confidence, while an ill-informed or naive one sometimes causes faith to waver. I knew a member of a bishopric who, while well meaning and affable in general, was skeptical and prejudiced toward learning. It caused him to come to the bishop or others constantly to ask even the most elementary questions about procedure and doctrine. It was evident that he studied little, a practice that left him vulnerable when it came to vital considerations for which he was almost always unprepared. It made it difficult for him to be an effective leader—not for lack of devotion to the gospel, but because he did not exude confidence to those around him.

One Primary president who was equally dedicated to the gospel and confident of her own opinions was terribly naive and uninformed. When she spoke about virtually any issue in a group, she betrayed her lack of preparation. Young people tittered in embarrassment, adults looked at each other in disbelief, and few sought her advice. It did not seem that she had ever read or digested a Church handbook or the scriptures.

It is perfectly acceptable, of course, for a leader to say, "I don't know," or to tell someone how to secure certain information; that is, after all, one of the clearest advantages of a good education. No one should assume that an education transforms a person into a walking encyclopedia, with an unlimited fund of knowledge at his or her grasp. Rather, an educated person knows of a wide variety of people, places, and ideas and can usually suggest sources of knowledge. Our obvious inability to know everything does not excuse us from working to attain knowledge. Even if we fall short of the goal of becoming as knowledgeable as we would like to be, we should make the attempt in order to gain confidence to lead effectively and to inspire others to trust us.

An unusually naive young couple joined the Church and a few weeks later began telephoning other members and inviting them to their home to listen to anti-Mormon instruction. This couple met some anti-Mormon zealots who were passing out pamphlets and holding meetings in an effort to persuade Mormons to leave the faith. The newly baptized members were immediately convinced by the arguments and began to proselyte against the Church also. Although most people who were contacted were not badly shaken in their faith, they were worried by arguments that they had never heard before. Because of the rapidly growing discontent in the ward, the bishop decided to take some positive action. Using the anti-Mormon literature as a foundation, he held a fireside for the adult members during which he considered the criticisms of the Mormon position, point by point. He examined the anti-Mormon sources and techniques so that the members would be familiar with them and could comfortably recognize similar sources and techniques in the future. He and the members considered all of the claims logically, and then compared them to historical fact based on a number of reliable sources.

On Sunday morning, the bishop took a similar approach with the young people, so that they could feel more confident about dealing with similar issues should they be confronted with them. They listened to a tape recording made by an anti-Mormon group, stopping it at strategic places to point out the fallacies of the argument and to explain the other side of the story. The reaction of both the adults and the young people was very positive. They had all heard enough about the topic that they were very interested in it, and they were very glad to be able to secure the information they thought they needed to deal intelligently with the problem. There were excellent discussions in both groups, and some people observed that the new information had a spiritual value that confirmed them in their own testimonies of the gospel.

Afterward, the anti-Mormon wave that had quickly swept the area faded noticeably. This very instructive experience suggested that people may not realize the need for knowledge until they have an urgent reason to use it. Similarly, new missionaries may learn the same thing the hard way when they are assigned to a first area in the mission and realize that they know too little about the gospel to talk intelligently about it. Missionaries may begin to study intensively only at this point, yet they were probably told many times by parents and teachers to prepare *before* their mission.

Misguided individuals sometimes suggest that Church members be discouraged from studying anything except the standard works for fear that some types of additional reading will threaten testimony. They may try to censor reading material that is readily available or even insist that people not read certain materials. This is an unfortunate approach, because it may cause people to think that their leaders are trying to hide the truth. As members of The Church of Jesus Christ of Latter-day Saints, we believe in and embrace all truth. Therefore, if people are well founded in knowledge, both spiritual and secular, they will be strong against temptation and falsehood. Anti-Mormon literature will not be convincing to people who are well grounded in the faith. Knowledge, rather than censorship, is the solution.

Realistically, there are certain aspects of world history, American history, or Mormon history that are unpleasant. The Mountain Meadows Massacre, for instance, is an unfortunate example of some early Mormons using violence against people they believed had been their persecutors in Missouri. Instead of trying to cover up this isolated incident, it is better to study it thoroughly, as well as the rest of our history, so that we can intelligently speak of this event as one episode that is uncharacteristic of our entire history. All religious groups have unsavory episodes in their past; they should admit to them honestly so that people can accept them for what they are.

If Joseph Smith made mistakes as a comparatively inexperienced young man who was given an enormous task in the restoration of the gospel and the organization of the Church, we should recognize that as realistic truth that helps us to appreciate him, his abilities, and his problems. Jesus said, "If ye continue in my word, then are ye my disciples indeed; and ye shall know the truth, and the truth shall make you free." (John 8:31, 32.) That process takes time.

Many of us have the habit of approaching the truth with caution, as if our followers could not bear all of it now, or as if it would actually be destructive. We teach our children just some of the truth, and we do the same with our students, those investigating the gospel, and our curious neighbors. Unwittingly, we may actually deny our followers a firm foundation of the gospel, and they will eventually lose confidence in us. In fact, the truth is liberating and strengthening. We should never be guilty of twisting it because we think our followers cannot bear it now, because when they discover what we have done they will not trust us. There is a significant difference in teaching systematically or gradually, and in teaching deceptively. Paul said we should give milk before meat; systematic teaching is effective as long as we are careful to give both the milk and the meat honestly and correctly. Emily Dickinson wrote an especially impressive poem that says it best:

> Tell all the Truth but tell it slant –
> Success in Circuit lies
> Too bright for our infirm Delight
> The truth's superb surprise

As lightening to the Children eased
With explanation kind
The Truth must dazzle gradually
Or every man be blind —[7]

The subtle sarcasm should awaken all of us to the necessity and desirability of facing truth squarely.

The Lord has great promises to those who serve him "in righteousness and in truth unto the end. Great shall be their reward and eternal shall be their glory. And to them will I reveal all mysteries, yea, all the hidden mysteries of my kingdom. . . . Yea, even the wonders of eternity shall they know, and things to come will I show them, even the things of many generations. And their wisdom shall be great, and their understanding reach to heaven. . . . For by my Spirit will I enlighten them, and by my power will I make known unto them the secrets of my will." (D&C 76:5-10.) Joseph Smith said: "God hath not revealed anything to Joseph, but what He will make known unto the Twelve, and even the least Saint may know all things as fast as he is able to bear them."[8]

Leaders sometimes rationalize away their lack of study by pointing to their heavy administrative burdens, but bureaucratic responsibilities will never substitute for the knowledge necessary to give advice at a critical time to a person in need. We all should consistently study to be prepared for any possible problem. Parents should not neglect studying scriptures with their families, because it establishes a pattern and helps children to know where the sources are and how to use them effectively. All family scripture reading sessions may not be equally valuable, but the pattern can be established and a standard taught. For family problems, it indicates to children that their parents are committed to seeking knowledge, and that without it they cannot lead effectively. "But to be learned is good if they hearken unto the counsels of God." (2 Nephi 9:29.)

Chapter Twelve

KEEPING LIFE IN BALANCE

When someone asks, "How do we do it all?," the simple answer is that we don't. We should realize that we don't have to do it all. Any leader must be a whole person in order to be effective in leadership as well as successful and happy in personal life. For all of us there are many voices demanding our time and energy, and we must choose which ones to obey. An effective leader cannot be a fanatic or a zealot who devotes all time and energy to one project, or one who regards himself as perfect enough to do every task without difficulty.

When asked how she responded to the injunction that she should be perfect, Pandy Warner, a prominent Utah educator, said: "I used to deal with it by not reading any publication written by a woman in the Church. I went through a phase where I would not open one up. I felt so intimidated by these women who could do everything and do it well. My major challenge was to get my children and me out the door at the same time in the morning. I was resentful toward women who were telling everyone they could handle it all. Then it dawned on me that perfection does not come all at once. I may be perfect in only one thing. I may be perfect in my sacrament meeting attendance for last Sunday. But it helps to do a tiny bit at a time because you get those pats on the back that carry you through. You've got to be able to accept within yourself that you're not going to be able to do everything. I gave up the notion of baking bread a long time ago. I don't sew. I tried that one time, and it took the fun out of my entire Christmas holidays. So I don't do that again, I'm learning. But arriving at your own perception of what perfection is is one key."[1]

Ruth Funk, former Young Women's general president, echoed this thought, noting that she has never baked a loaf of bread in her life. She used to feel guilty about it. "But homemaking [as traditionally perceived] wasn't where I wanted to spend my time, although I found that nurturing and loving my husband and children brought my greatest joy. But I loved reading and teaching. And from the beginning of our marriage I continually responded to and accepted civic and Church callings."[2]

Barbara Winder came at the problem from a slightly different direction. Instead of worrying about those things she has not accomplished, she believes in taking pride in what she has accomplished. "I remember one day when my children were young. They had been ill, and I hadn't been able to accomplish any of the routine things I would have liked. The house was not at all orderly, and I was not feeling at all lovely. When my husband came home that night, I told him, 'I feel like a failure today; I've been caring for the children and haven't done what I wanted to get done.' He said, 'Tell me the things that you have done today.' I enumerated the things that I had done, and then my husband said, 'I want you to think about *those* things, not about the things you *haven't* done.' I think we all need to use that philosophy more in our lives."[3]

Continuing in the same vein, Sister Winder said: "Sometimes we go through a period of trying to do everything all at once. I have had people tell me, 'Oh, you've done so many things' and I tell them 'But I've lived so many years!' *There really is a season for everything.* I couldn't possibly do today what I am doing as Relief Society General President if my children were small and still at home and I were caring for them. My emphasis is a bit different now, though my priority is still with my husband and family.

"This is a lesson we all have to learn. Only we can judge how much we can handle. We often think that someone else is doing everything. But usually one sister is doing one thing, and another sister is doing something else, and yet another sister is doing another thing. Then we try to do it all! And when it all comes tumbling down around our feet we realize that we *can't* do it all. As we learn what we can do, we are growing; and then sometimes we can take on a little more—perhaps because of what we have learned in the process."[4]

When I lived in a university ward as a married college student in Salt Lake City, our bishop was an unusual man named Jay Jensen. Although he always seemed to me to be remarkably effective in what he did, he always carried with him a certain calm, a serenity or peace of mind that gave me confidence. He never seemed harried. He was always capable of giving people his full attention. Suggesting that a bishop's job was so demanding that it was almost impossible, I once asked him how he "did it all." "No one does," he said. "It is a matter of balance." He said that it was a mistake for anyone to give up his family because of an important Church calling, and he made sure that he continued to have the time he needed to spend with his young family. He simply drew the line at participation in some Church activities, allowing his counselors to stand in for him. He asserted that it was a matter of choosing those things that were most important at any given time.

When I was called to be a bishop myself, my stake president gave my children admirable advice. He said that if I was not spending enough time with them, they were to call him on the telephone and he would promise to release me—even if I had only served eighteen months! (The last phrase was lighthearted reference to my own assertion that every other call I had held in the Church had lasted only eighteen months.) My children were impressed, and several times they threatened me with that directive. It served a useful role in keeping my activities outside the home in perspective. This stake president aptly illustrated the well-known LDS axiom that the well-being of the family should always come first, no matter what the calling. It is important for every married couple to strike the right balance between Church activity and time for marriage and family.

In an article about reducing stress, Eric Stephan, a professor of interpersonal communication, advised the need for establishing peace of mind, praying, eating and sleeping properly, and exercising. Finally, he added, "Don't be disappointed because you can't do everything. And don't compete against everybody and everything. If you try too hard, you will surely lose the most important race of your own life—the race toward peaceful and joyful living." He encouraged people to ask themselves the question, "Who will even know or care in a hundred years?" as a helpful way of separating the truly important things from those that are of lesser importance.

According to Dr. Stephen, it is wise to concentrate on one thing at a time, combining your own resources and abilities with those of other people. Then you should "treat yourself" after accomplishing something with a relaxing activity: an evening walk, a hot bath, a great salad, some relaxing music, some humor, a two hour vacation, or any number of other possibilities that will promote peace of mind. He reminded us that we are never "required to run faster or labor more than our strength and means." (Mosiah 4:27.)[5]

After being told following a physical examination that my blood pressure was on the borderline between high and normal, I inaugurated a vigorous exercise program, combining calisthenics and cycling with a daily three-mile brisk walk. At first I resented the time lost from my professional pursuits, thinking of all the things I could be doing if I were at my desk. But when I realized how much the exercise relaxed me, how much better I felt, and how much easier it was to control my weight, I decided it was actually time gained. Some of the best thinking and planning I do occurs during my exercise time. Now I try very hard to guard that exercise time, because it seems to make me a more balanced and more optimistic person, as well as a healthier one.

Any leader has to take time to feed his own soul: to read scriptures, to pray, to ponder, or to teach the family. It seems equally important to make time in life for fun, leisure, relaxation, and diversion. A person who does so may be a better leader in a variety of ways. Recently, Marti and I found ourselves overcome with responsibilties. Our stake callings in the Church necessitated our going to wards other than our own on Sundays, while our children chose to go by themselves to our ward. We were so busy the rest of the day that we had no time to unwind, to enjoy the Sabbath, to do for others, or to reflect on the things of the gospel. We were leaving our children too much to their own devices. We were too insistent on achieving in professional matters. The need for balance became painfully evident. We decided that we needed to be more devoted to fun and relaxation.

As a result, we made a pact to relax more and continued to remind each other constantly of that need. On a Father's Day card, Marti wrote to me: "Here's to having *more fun* this coming year than we did last year!" We found it necessary sometimes to say no to an invitation to Church work and instead to run off to a movie. But it is still difficult. Recently, after attending a friend's baptism, we decided to do something that seemed wild and crazy. "Let's go to a movie!" We determined that there were two movies that we would like to see, but when we arrived at the first one we found that it started later than we hoped and would not be over until midnight. So we drove to the other theater and discovered that it did not start for another hour and would not be over until ten minutes *after* midnight. Although we were interested in fun, we were also getting more tired by the minute. Finally, we opted for two Snickers candy bars and went home. It is never easy to maintain balance. The truth seems to be that when one is constantly busy or devoted to a cause, it is very difficult to ease up and have fun. We almost don't know how.

Quinn McKay once wrote a fascinating article about what he called "Principles in Conflict," a phenomenon he defined as "two righteous principles" confronting "a person in such a way that if he is to obey one principle, he will be forced to violate another. These are really difficult kinds of decisions that cause loss of sleep, guilt feelings, and worry." In other words, there may be no absolutely correct answer. Adam and Eve, for instance, were told to multiply and replenish the earth and yet not to partake of the fruit of the tree of knowledge of good and evil. To obey one commandment required the violation of the other. As Lehi said, "For it must needs be, that there is an opposition in all things." (2 Nephi 2:11.)

One example McKay offered is a father who promised his son, a cub scout, that he would attend a pack meeting. In the meantime, a government official calls the father to meet with the governor at the airport to translate conversations with a dignitary from a foreign country. One principle is that the father should keep his promise to his son, and the second is that he should be responsive to his duty to community and country.

Another example is about a man who is employed by a store owner who decides to do business on the Sabbath day. It is possible for the man to get another job, but he would have to take a twenty percent pay cut. The family determines that although it would be difficult, they could survive financially on a lower salary. According to Quinn McKay, it is important to remember whenever principles seem to collide that we should choose to obey the higher law. Marion D. Hanks once said, "Never let things which matter most be at the mercy of things which matter least."[6]

In a similar example, Carolyn Rasmus remembered a statement by Ardeth Kapp that says: "The adversary would keep us distracted from the few vital things that matter as we keep busy with many trivial things that make little difference." Sister Rasmus went on to say: "We are very much a doing kind of people. This last week a group of women in my ward got together and tied a quilt for a friend whose mother passed away. Afterwards they were talking about what a wonderful conversation they'd had, and one of them said, 'Isn't it interesting, I'd never come if somebody said we were just going to sit and talk.' But it seemed okay that we came to quilt, as if somehow the activity . . . legitimizes us pursuing some things. We have a group of women in our ward who walk every day. They're called the traveling synagogue because they all study the scriptures while they walk. I asked one woman, 'Would you feel comfortable if you met every afternoon and studied the scriptures,' and she said she wouldn't. Now that's a terrible indictment for us. If we measure everything in terms of doing, perhaps we don't equate the idea of learning or some of the things that really do matter as being important. And I think that's part of the perfecting kind of process. We could keep busy all the time with things that don't matter at all."[7]

Francine Bennion illustrated this point by referring to the life of Christ: "Christ recognizes the seeming contradictions, the constant tension between opposites in this life, even tension between two 'goods'—not just the tension between good and evil, but tensions between the very matters of existence. He turns the tensions upside down to illustrate them: for example, 'Whosoever shall seek to save his life shall lose it; and whosoever shall lose his life shall preserve it.' (Luke 17:33) or, 'But he that is greatest among you shall be your servant.' (Matt. 23:11.) That pattern repeatedly suggests that for Christ the ways in which his people perceived things and their opposites were not necessarily the only ways or even the most useful ways.

"Frequently he was invited to sit on the horns of a dilemma, to be trapped in an either/or proposition. Again and again he would transcend both horns with a principle that embraced them both. (For example, see Mark 12:13-17. 'Render to Caesar the things that are Caesar's and to God the things that are God's.') He simplifies and clarifies matters without, it seems to me, implying that existence itself is simple.[8]

Our own choices may often be between two "goods" requiring our discernment as to which is the higher law or the best one for us to make at that time. There are many times when we should make a choice, instead of supposing that we must do everything. Any job is best understood if we view it in increments or stages. If one takes a position of leadership—in church, in the family, or in the world—one is bound to realize that it is impossible to complete all the tasks listed in the job description.

As a new bishop, I became depressed as I read the seemingly never-ending list of tasks that were included in my job description. Although I tried to organize my time so as to accomplish all of it, I belatedly realized that it was impossible. Rather, I would be more successful if I focused on certain tasks of high priority, worked hard at them, and then afterward went on to a second group of tasks. I was able to delegate many responsibilities to others and to decide that certain ones could wait for my attention. Afterward, I was much more secure in the realization that the leaders of the Church did not in fact expect me to accomplish all those things—at least not at once!

We have to apply the same principle in our homes and with our families. There are certain jobs inside and outside the home that are accomplished only on an incremental or alternate basis. (Marti just painted the kitchen—the first time we have done it in eleven years!) Some of our tasks are too low on the list of priorities, and so we never get around to doing them. Even though our families are our most important responsibilities, we can easily decide that even all the things we would like to do with them cannot be accomplished at once either. We have to decide what things are most important and focus on those first.

During his senior year of high school, our oldest son Darrin began applying to universities. We soon realized that many other family needs would take a back seat for a while. We needed to spend time with him talking about the various schools and visiting some of them. Then there were applications and essays to write, advice to give, and finally a choice of universities to be made. It was Darrin's decision to be made, but he needed advice and support. During those months of activity, some of our other children undoubtedly felt that Darrin was receiving undue attention as compared to their own. But this was equivalent to putting out a fire or handling a crisis, and we had to face it. The other children will require similar concentrated periods of attention in their own lives, which will also interrupt the balance.

Many of us may also find the need to spend a great deal of time on a Church activity for some weeks, then equal time to a professional task, then to a family task. My high council responsibilities once placed me in charge of an education series that lasted two days, during which members of our stake would participate in classes and lectures about a variety of issues. We brought some speakers into our stake from across the country and also utilized some very talented people who lived in the boundaries of our stake. There were some very concentrated periods of activity during the planning of this series, and then a very concentrated week of activity when the event actually occurred. During that time my family saw comparatively little of me, and we all breathed a sigh of relief when it was over. It was hard, but we did it. It was worth doing, but it caused some of our normal activities to suffer. Afterward, we re-emphasized time with the family to try to redress the balance.

In her free-lance editorial work, Marti has the need for certain periods of concentrated work so that she can meet deadlines. During that period of two or three weeks, the family has to rely less on her than is their usual practice. We don't care much for the pressure and neither does she, but we all realize that this work is necessary and that she will be with us again, with her full attention, when it is over. When I finish a book or article, or come to the end of a semester and find myself reading papers and exams in order to assign grades to my students, I experience similar periods. My time then is very limited for other activities.

None of our lives are likely to maintain a perfect, regular balance. Some things will require a great deal of attention and then other things will consume us; then we may even have a period when we can actually live moderately. In all of this activity, we need to remember: "The things that matter most should never be at the mercy of the things that matter least."

Chapter Thirteen

WHEN LEADERSHIP CHANGES HANDS

Neal Maxwell once said: "It should be clear to us with regard to various callings and assignments that just as soon as we are sustained and set apart the clock begins running toward the moment of our release. How vital it is to manage our time and talents wisely from the moment a task begins. Later, when we have devotedly invested much of ourselves in a particular calling or assignment (and especially when it has been satisfying and we have made a real difference), we may feel the release when it comes, but that, too, is part of our schooling as disciples. Being released gives us experience in patience and humility, as well as a fresh reminder of our non-essentiality."[1]

Admittedly, people need to exercise humility toward their leadership callings and be willing to relinquish them at the appropriate time, to be willing to accept change. By the same token, those who succeed other people need to do so with humanity and sensitivity, insuring an effective and desirable transition. Releasing and sustaining involves human beings much more than it does programs. It is vital, therefore, that we do not treat the "change of the guard" in a political or superficial fashion.

When politicians from the opposing party are elected to office, their immediate tendency is to sweep the slate clean—to fire all the appointees left from the predecessor. We think of this as the spoils of office, and most political appointees expect it. If a Republican is elected governor, he most certainly will fire all Democrats (and vice versa), and will bring on board hand-picked people, all of whom will probably be Republicans. While this is politically common, a politician is well advised to think carefully before replacing his staff. Even given political considerations, there may be highly qualified, experienced people who would be extremely valuable to the newly elected politician and equally loyal. In any "change of the guard" it is a mistake to arbitrarily sweep all previous appointees from office.

This is an even more important concept in church leadership, where we must exercise patience and long suffering, and give people a chance even if they are not our favorites. Every new leader should be patient about making changes. Joe Christensen said: "Before making sweeping revolutionary changes, be sure you have made a sincere investment of personal time and study in order to understand the scope and nature of the new assignment. Be patient enough to pay that kind of price. The other day I heard the counsel, 'Before knocking down a wall, remember that somebody must have had a reason for putting it there in the first place. It not only weakens an organization, but many times can be a source of real embarrassment when someone new in a position of responsibility moves decisively and makes some sweeping change that he later regrets.[2]

One bishop demonstrated all the dreaded impatience that Joe Christensen warned against. He was relatively new in the Church, was a political zealot, and tended to interpret religious loyalty similarly to political loyalty. Because he disagreed with much of what the previous bishop had done, he thought that anyone previously called to positions should be released. So he unceremoniously swept from office all of the key leaders of the ward, including one who had only served three months and was doing an admirable job. He explained to the ward in a sacrament meeting that it was necessary for him to have people with whom he could work effectively, implying that he could not work with *all* members of the ward. The effect on the congregation was chilling. Shocked and hurt, many people extended only grudging support.

The long-term impact on the ward was considerable. There was an increase in gossip, a loss of amiability and desire to serve, and a lack of cohesiveness that permeated the entire membership. Although the bishop did not realize the seriousness of his actions, they were discussed at great length at meetings of the stake high council.

One day during sacrament meeting, one high councilor took the liberty of standing during testimony meeting in an effort to smooth over the hard feelings. He suggested that different bishops had different styles and meant no harm in carrying out their programs. He said that members should exercise patience in judging the effectiveness of those actions. At the same time, he avowed his faith in slow, careful change, done only with fasting and prayer and on a case-by-case basis.

Once during an eloquent sermon on leadership, Elder Matthew Cowley said that we need to be careful about the way "we release people from their positions—not only in this organization, but in all organizations of the Church. We must not hurt people, remember that; therefore, we must be very careful, very diplomatic, and do it after praying when it becomes necessary to release teachers and other officers in your organization. It certainly is not fair for it to be announced in a stake conference or in some other meeting that 'so and so is released,' when he has not heard about it before. To me that is insulting. We should be just as careful and considerate of the person we are releasing from a position as we are of a person we are calling into a position in the Church."

Elder Cowley went on to say: "Get close to your teachers, know them intimately, know their problems, get their viewpoints, have understanding hearts. Know your board members, know them personally and intimately, and even where personalities may clash, always remember that in the work of God there must be no clash, but rather harmony, appreciation for one another, and sustaining one another. Do not let your personalities impede the work of God."[3]

It is a common temptation for someone succeeding to an office to notice all the policies or procedures with which he disagrees and then issue profound criticism. Usually, a leader does not share such criticism with members at large, but may do so with other Church leaders in executive meetings, saying just enough to indicate to those listening that the new leader does not approve of the former leader's programs and procedures. New leaders are often guilty of making the following comments: "I can't imagine why she wanted to adopt that ineffective program." "This never should have been done in the first place—it is contrary to Church procedure." "I can't believe the shape things were in when I was called!" or "I don't know how people could survive that kind of leadership."

Every leader should be understanding and appreciative enough of his predecessor to applaud the performance at every opportunity and resist any temptation to criticize. According to Dr. Christensen, a successor who condemns or criticizes a predecessor in the presence of those who served with that person will find that approximately half of them are loyal to the predecessor and alienated toward the successor. Even if someone agrees with the expressed views, his sense of fair play may preclude supporting the new leader. It is an obvious sign of maturity for a leader to be able to acknowledge or recognize the achievement of others.[4]

A new leader can benefit greatly from the experience and wisdom of a former one, and it is therefore to his advantage to pay respect and be willing to accord deserved commendation. More important than than, it is an integral part of the gospel. "Judge not, that ye be not judged." (Matthew 7:1.) "Be ye therefore merciful, as your Father also is merciful." (Luke 6:36.) "Leave judgment alone with me, for it is mine and I will repay. Peace be with you; my blessings continue with you." (D&C 83:23.)

There may be numerous opportunities in the first months of service for a new leader to call on the former leader and ask advice about specific problems. If their differing styles seem to dictate differing decisions, advice may still be indispensable from someone who knows more about a certain person or situation, or has made numerous similar decisions. Asking former leaders for advice, then listening intently, will often pay real dividends in making effective leaders. "What do you think of this problem? Did you know this person very well? How did you handle this situation?" Those questions never lock the successor into a prescribed pattern, and in most cases, the predecessor does not know what action is finally taken; yet the successor can benefit from the experience of the predecessor.

I remember one potentially embarrassing problem. A welfare project had been initiated by the previous bishop only a few months before he left office, and I inherited it. It was a bee-keeping, honey-raising project, and I knew nothing about bees. One of my first tasks was to lose myself in literature about bees and to talk to other ward leaders about the project. Not surprisingly, I discovered that the person who knew the most about bee-keeping was the previous bishop.

Unfortunately, the man to whom the bishop delegated the bee-keeping project was about to move from the ward. The bishop was now busy in the stake presidency. No one knowledgeable was available to head the operation. After a lot of soul-searching and praying, I decided to end our involvement in the project. I tried to do so without suggesting any rancor toward the previous bishop, for whom I had great respect, but only on the grounds that this project seemed inadvisable. For the previous bishop I was sure it would have worked and would have been successful, for he had a track record of successes that was almost unparalleled. But for me, the project seemed headed for disaster. When I made the decision I immediately told my predecessor about it, so that I would be sure there was no misunderstanding. He received the news in a very generous, tolerant way, assuring me that he knew that the project we embraced would have to be one that was comfortable for us. I felt relief and valued his support, which he always gave enthusiastically.

Joe Christensen expressed it well: "When you want to innovate or effect a change in policy or procedure, seek as broad a base of consensus or support among those affected as possible. In other words, let the idea have a 'life of its own.' Talk about it. Get responses, suggestions, adaptations. The decision can become a group decision which almost everyone will support when some of the 'IH-Factor' (Invented Here) is included."[5]

Many Church leaders are so fearful that people will disagree with their ideas that they feel they must formulate them secretly and then formally announce them as accomplished facts. They expect members to accept them unconditionally as a signal of their loyalty and obedience. They worry excessively about "leaks" before the announcement is made, the same way government officials frequently worry about premature announcements of their programs. Actually, discussion about proposed programs brings greater unity afterward and irons out possible problems prior to their enactment. People always support policies and programs more devotedly if they believe that they played a role in their formulation.

In my early months of service as a bishop, some of us determined that our parking lot would have to be expanded because of increasing attendance at meetings causing an overflow of cars on a narrow street. A committee studied the issue and presented a proposal to the bishopric, and we investigated costs as well as our ability to pay. We found that we had enough money in our building fund to finish the project without asking for any individual donations. Then I proposed that we discuss it with the membership before taking formal action. Interestingly enough, one member of the bishopric objected and forcefully argued that I should not discuss it at all, but rather should announce it as a *fait accompli* and then ask for a sustaining vote, making it a kind of loyalty test to the bishop. I resisted that reasoning, feeling that people would feel better about the project if they could discuss it openly.

At our next meeting we discussed it, and there were a few strongly expressed opinions that we should not do it, some because it would deplete our building funds for the eventual construction of a cultural hall and classroom wing, and others because of aesthetic considerations. I remained convinced that it was the best option, and we went ahead with the project, receiving the support of those few people who had expressed opposition. They respected the way we had approached the project even though they disagreed with the final decision.

A new leader should avoid discussing with anyone the supposed weaknesses of his predecessor. As Dr. Christensen said, "So often, what we exhibit in this kind of action is really insecurity within ourselves in allowing someone else his right to do things differently. Often the differences really are matters of preference or policy, and not principle. Good men and women have been unjustly criticized for having merely been different in their style of operation, while they espouse almost the identical basic righteous principles of their successor."[6]

In one ward a Young Women's president was succeeded by an experienced person who seemed to be twice as effective. Under the first president, the Young Women's program languished. The young women failed to identify with her, were uncomfortable in her presence, did not trust her with their problems, and were shocked to find that she was a shy and ineffective speaker. She was also so disorganized that many individuals suffered and parents began to complain. Conversely, the woman who replaced her had all the right gifts of leadership. She was organized, sincerely interested in the young women, and she had an infectious enthusiasm. They young women were so encouraged that they could barely hide their happiness. It was obvious to the entire ward that this was a needed change, and that the new president was fulfilling her role in a very successful way. But she never discussed her predecessor's weaknesses; instead, she tried in various ways to honor her and pay tribute to certain accomplishments that she could sincerely talk about. At an evening held to honor the young women and their parents, the new president made a special presentation to the former president and praised the work she had done. She did not have to behave in this discreet, sensitive way, because she had all the support she needed from parents and youth. Yet she did it to demonstrate Christian love and concern for her predecessor.

One bishop, stake president, elders quorum president, Relief Society president, or Young Women's president may be highly organized and a polished executive. His successor may be strong on people skills but not particularly gifted with details. Which one is the best? Our individual prejudice may lead us to favor one of these over another, but who is to say that one is better than the other? They are simply different styles of leadership that may serve people equally well.

I knew an impressive Relief Society president who was smooth in manner, articulate, and authoritative. She was a woman who was always in the right place at the right time. She was outgoing and involved and seemed to have an answer for every problem. She gave effective talks based on personal experience and filled them with anecdotes that kept her followers enthralled. Her successor was a shy woman, characterized more than anything else by her humility and the love and compassion she demonstrated for others. She always passed up opportunities to speak, and when she did speak, it was not very memorable. But she lent a considerable presence to all events, and people thought of her as Christlike. The members had great respect for both women and loved both for very different reasons.

Parents frequently exemplify similar contrasts. Marti's

father is a dynamic, gregarious man, a fluent speaker and gifted organizer, who commands instant respect from people who know him as well as from his children. My father was a quiet, gentle, unassuming man, who enjoyed people but did not like to be the center of attention. His obviously unselfish manner and willingness to help others to the sacrifice of his own personal well-being always endeared him to his friends and family. Who is to say which style is the best or which parent would produce the most enviable offspring?

Leaders are people with all the human frailties and positive qualities that make their contributions dynamic. If leadership could be exercised by a machine it could, theoretically, perform in flawless style, with precision and with predictability. The product would be static. A human being brings diverse characteristics based on heredity and environment, on personality and education, on experiences and philosophy, as well as the guidance of the Spirit. Providing leaders accept the guidance of the Spirit, they can be effective in spite of diversity, and successful and dynamic because of it.

Chapter Fourteen

LEADING BY THE SPIRIT

To lead effectively, we have to be sensitive to the guidance of the Spirit. The prophet Enos illustrated enviable determination when he knelt before the Lord "all the day long" and when the night came he still raised his "voice high that it reached the heavens." After that long, difficult process, the Lord responded by telling Enos his sins were forgiven, and Enos proclaimed that his "faith began to be unshaken in the Lord." (Enos 4-12.)

Dwan Young, general Primary president, said: "Your prayer can take many forms. It can be sung in a hymn, or whispered, or even thought. It can be as short as one word—'help!'—or it could be as long as Enos's prayer that lasted all night and all day. . . . The important thing to remember is that he can guide you. When you draw near to Heavenly Father in prayer, he will draw near to you. You need never feel alone again."[1]

When Church leaders challenge their followers to pray for even five minutes at a time, many realize that they are actually spending very little time in prayer. Just as no one-sided conversation can be satisfying, a prayer must include time for listening. The Prophet Joseph Smith said, "Yea, thus saith the still small voice; which whispereth through and pierceth all things, and often times it maketh my bones to quake while it maketh manifest." (D&C 85:6.)

The Lord tried to explain the process to Joseph. "Yea, behold, I will tell you in your mind and in your heart, by the Holy Ghost, which shall come unto you and which shall dwell in your heart. Now behold, this is the spirit of revelation." (D&C 8:2-3.) Joseph then wrote: "A person may profit by noticing the first intimation of the spirit of revelation; for instance, when you feel pure intelligence flowing into you, it may give you sudden strokes of ideas, so that by noticing it, you may find it fulfilled the same day or soon; those things that were presented into your minds by the spirit of God, will come to pass and thus by learning the Spirit of God and understanding it, you may grow into the principle of revelation until you become perfect in Jesus Christ."[2]

Speaking to Joseph Smith and the leaders of the Church, the Lord said, "And this is the ensample unto them, that they shall speak as they are moved upon by the Holy Ghost.

"And whatsoever they shall speak when moved upon by the Holy Ghost shall be scripture, shall be the will of the Lord, shall be the voice of the Lord, and the power of God unto salvation." (D&C 68:3-4.) The Lord encourages leaders to be sensitive to the Spirit.

Bruce R. McConkie once said: "Every devoted, obedient, and righteous person on earth has and does receive revelation from God. Revelation is the natural inheritance of all the faithful."[3]

When Connie Woolstenhulme was called to be Relief Society president in her Ricks College ward in Idaho, she was most nervous about selecting her counselors. She said: "I wondered how I would know if my choices were right. How would I know if the Lord was answering my prayers? It took me a long time. It was just through prayer. There were so many girls I knew would do a good job. I had chosen one counselor and felt good about her. Then I got stuck.

"It was the morning I was supposed to turn the names in to the bishop. I was looking out this window at the apartments in our dorm complex. I mentally kept going through who lived in which apartment. Suddenly this girl's name came into my mind. I knew she was the one to be my other counselor. Somehow I had just overlooked her before. She was wonderful."[4]

Although it is often not fully understood by many, fasting acts as a catalyst for spiritual guidance, speeding up the process of communication from God through prayer. Yet many people approach it with hesitation. A friend once told me cynically: "All fasting accomplishes is to make me hungry." In fact, the simplicity of that statement reveals the true worth of the process. When we fast and pray about a problem, we may be reminded continually throughout the day of the reason for the fast by recurring hunger pangs. As a result, prayer is entered into consistently until an answer is received. Fasting is effective for many people because it frees them from concentration on their own immediate needs and allows them to focus on those of others.

When Oliver Cowdery had difficulty translating, the Lord explained to him a simple process by which he could recognize answer to prayer. "You must study it out in your mind; then you must ask me if it be right, and if it is right I will cause that your bosom shall burn within you; therefore, you shall feel that it is right." But, the Lord continued, "if it be not right you shall have no such feelings, but you shall have a stupor of thought that shall cause you to forget the thing which is wrong." (D&C 9:8-9.)

Although when I was growing up I was unsure of the ultimate difference between a "burning in the bosom" and a "stupor of thought," the straightforward formula appealed to me. As a high school student, I determined that I would act on this advice and obtain my own testimony of the gospel. I wanted to "know" that it was true. I carefully read the Book of Mormon, underlining as I went, making notes about memorable passages. When I finished I felt a great sense of anticipation about Moroni's promise. Kneeling in prayer, I tried to learn for myself whether this book was true or not. Although I prayed intermittently for several weeks with what I thought was "real intent" and determination, I failed to recognize an answer. When my friends stood in fast meeting to express their testimonies, my parents were disappointed that I did not. I could not be dishonest, so I told them that I was trying, but that a testimony had thus far eluded me. I worried and wondered what I was doing wrong. Perhaps my life was not good enough for the Lord to recognize my efforts; maybe there was something wrong with the method I was using to pray; or I just did not know how to recognize an answer that may already have come.

For two more years I continued to study and pray. I reread the Book of Mormon. Finally, I received a call from my bishop to serve a mission. On one hand, I was elated because I had wanted to serve; but on the other hand, I was worried because the lack of testimony would make me an ineffective advocate. Although my brother was going on a mission at the same time, my parents, who were people of very modest means, enthusiastically pledged themselves to our financial support.

In my interview with the stake president, he surprised me by suggesting that to lessen the financial burden on my parents, I should stay at home until my older brother returned. Greatly disappointed, I returned home to tell my father. Normally a quiet, soft-spoken man, he fervently argued that I should go at the same time as my brother, and that the Lord would help us to meet the financial obligations. Dad put on his coat and announced that he was going to talk with the stake president. "You are going on a mission—and you are going now!" he said, with a conviction I had never seen in him before. Then kneeling in family prayer, my father uttered a simple, short prayer, expressing thanks for blessings, asking for help in his conversation with the stake president and for help for his sons as they prepared to leave on missions.

As I listened with faith to that prayer and tried to look into the future, I was spiritually moved beyond anything I can describe. At that instant, I received my testimony of the truthfulness of the gospel. I was overcome with a feeling of happiness and excitement and was confident that my father could persuade the stake president that we should both go. I knew absolutely that I would be able to go on a mission and testify with honesty and certainty to anyone who would listen to me. It was an enormously satisfying experience. My previous anxieties were gone. My father succeeded in his talk with the stake president, and my parents not only subsequently supported two missionaries but they prospered financially as they never had before.

I have tried to analyze the possible reasons that it took me so long to gain a testimony. Whatever they were, the timing helped to increase my faith in my Heavenly Father as well as my earthly father. Although I didn't expect to see a vision as Joseph Smith did, I wasn't sure if I would recognize a burning in the bosom either. As it turned out, I recognized the answer when it came very clearly. The Lord told Joseph that He spoke to his servants "in their weakness, after the manner of their language, that they might come to understanding." (D&C 1:24.)

Everyone feels and describes their spiritual experiences differently. Maybe I needed to learn how the Lord would speak to me and recognize the answers I was getting. I understand now. When I pray for an answer, I use the same formula taught to me in my youth. I study it out in my mind, make what I think is a reasoned decision, then I ask the Lord if it is right. If it is right, I feel a growing sense of excitement until I am convinced that the Lord approves of the decision. When I am fasting, the lack of food continually reminds me of the purpose. I pray frequently and feel a surging excitement and certainty as if the Holy Ghost had given an impression to my soul. If it is wrong, I become confused and depressed, and I know that I am experiencing a "stupor of thought."

I am convinced that the Lord will answer our prayers, but we have to communicate with him enough that we recognize how he talks to us. We have to get to know him. Once we have received that warm assurance that comes when a prayer is answered, when we receive a spiritual witness, we will understand how communication with God occurs. Joseph F. Smith described the impressions of the Spirit on his soul as so impressive that he felt it "from the crown of his head to the soles of his feet. God has shown it to me and removed all doubt from my mind, and I accept it as I accept the fact that the sun shines at midday."[5]

Loren C. Dunn of the Quorum of Seventy said, "It may not come like a flash of light (I don't know how the Lord is going to communicate with you), more than likely it will be the reassurance, a feeling in your heart, a reaffirmation that will come in a rather calm, natural but real way from day to day until you come to a realization that you *do* know."[6] And on another occasion he said, "I will tell you one thing—you will not gain a knowledge of the things of God on an instantaneous basis."[7]

Dwan Young recounted her use of prayer for answers in her Primary calling, to care for the children of the Church and all the world. She could only feel the burden of her calling initially, and needed the help of the Lord constantly. She prayed for the leaders around the world, that the Spirit of the Lord would help them to love children and understand them. She prayed for parents to love and teach their children: "Then just the other morning, I thought, 'I have been asking for so much. This morning I am not going to ask for one thing. I'm just going to be grateful.' I knelt and thanked the Lord for my good health, for my understanding husband, for our children, for our missionary son, for the privilege of serving, for the board members and staff who assist me, for stake and ward members throughout the world who are serving, and especially for the teachers who give and care so much. I thanked him for the children everywhere. I thanked him for the prophet. And the list went on. My spirit soared. What an astounding experience to know that I have so much! It takes a grateful heart to experience that soaring, that realization of how much Heavenly Father loves you, how much he does for you."[8]

It was clear to me in growing up that my dad led his home by the power of the Spirit. Even before he uttered the prayer that helped me to get my testimony, he knew what was supposed to happen in the life of his family, and he was determined to see it come true. There were other times when I felt the unmistakable impression that he was speaking by the Spirit. Sometimes he would say, "I feel we should do this" or "I feel that you should not go." I came to recognize those times when he spoke with conviction.

Marti and I have had similar experiences in our own family. When our oldest son was very young, we were returning home from a Utah visit, and intended to view the Hill Cumorah Pageant on our last day of travel. It was July and the days had been very hot. By the time we reached Palmyra, with the temperature in the high nineties, Darrin was suffering from heatstroke. I had made advance motel reservations, and we drove directly there, intending to take him inside to cool off. But as I drove, I had a very strong spiritual impression that I should choose the motel across the street instead. Intellectually, that seemed ridiculous because our reservations were at the first motel, so I drove to the motel that had our reservations. When I talked to the desk clerk, he claimed that he had no record of our reservations and that every room was taken. I pleaded with him because of the condition of our son, but to no avail. Quickly, I jumped into the car and drove across the street and successfully obtained a room that had just been vacated.

Once, while Darrin was playing Church softball as a teenager and running for a base, he was hit by a ball on the ear; it cut him deeply. Although his hearing did not seem to be affected, there was considerable bleeding. Because of the pain he felt when we touched it, we were unable to tell exactly where the cut was centered. Reason dictated that stitches were not required medically and that a scar on the ear would not be a cosmetic problem. But I felt a strong impression that Darrin should go the hospital emergency room. He and I drove to the hospital, and when the cut was exposed I could see a very deep, long opening in his ear. It was evident to the physician that stitches, eight in all would be required.

Not too long ago, I had profound spiritual experience while sitting in my high priests quorum on Sunday morning. At the end of the meeting, a new teacher was to be sustained and set apart. Before the blessing, I had a very strong impression that I would be asked to offer the benediction to the meeting, and then I literally saw in my mind the words that I should say. They were written as if in a script and unrolled quickly before my eyes. The prayer to be uttered seemed very close to a blessing for this new teacher's health.

It so happened that he was a close friend of mine, and he had been suffering a severe health problem, causing him intense pain and suffering. The prayer I was to give asked for the blessing of the Lord on his health as it would relate to his spiritual calling. I was surprised and nervous, and wondered if it was really appropriate to pray in public about a matter that was really very private. This man did not broadcast his problems to others and had only told me about them in confidence. Yet the impression was clear. Only a minute or two later, the high priests group leader turned to me and asked me to offer the closing prayer. I arose and uttered the prayer that seemed prepared for me in advance, and I felt the unmistakable guidance of the Spirit. When it was over, I was so overcome that I went to my friend and confided the story to him, telling him that I thought it was an impressive example of the Lord's interest and concern for his health.

In Church leadership too I have felt the guidance of the Spirit. One day while sitting on the stand during a sacrament service, I felt a strong impression. From the stand, I could see a man I knew well, a nonmember of the Church, who usually attended church with his wife and family. He was an avid supporter of the Church and his family in their callings. As I looked at him, I felt impelled to challenge him to be baptized. This seemed ridiculous because it was so much against my nature. Approaching friends about the gospel has always been difficult for me, and I am much more likely to drag my feet. For some reason, it seemed imperative that I give this man a strong message right away, perhaps so that he could be prepared to succeed me as a bishop.

At the end of the meeting, I rushed up the aisle and invited him to talk. When we were alone, I candidly explained my feelings. I told him that it was my conviction that he should study the gospel and pray and join the Church right away, because the Lord had a great work for him to do. He listened attentively, and seemed complimented rather than offended. He said that he had great respect for my opinions, and that he would consider the conversation seriously. We have remained great friends since that day, but at this writing he has not yet joined the Church. Nevertheless, I have hope. Following that conversation I felt overwhelming relief and peace in the knowledge that I had acted as the Lord directed.

On another occasion I had an unusual experience following a bishopric meeting. I had met with my counselors to discuss the calling of a ward finance clerk. Previously we had two clerks, neither of whom was comfortable or competent in the position. The bishopric talked about several people, finally focusing on one man we agreed would be effective in the calling. As I got into my car and drove out of the parking lot, another name was, it seemed, inserted into my mind as though viewed on a television screen. It was a name we had not discussed because the brother was serving on the high council. I knew without any question that he should be called. It seemed that the Lord was determined to prevent me from making a serious mistake. Unknown to me at the time, this man was about to be released from the high council and therefore would be available. Fortunately, we were able to make the call a reality, he did a wonderful job, and the experience taught me that the Lord selects his own and inspires his leaders.

Even though I never envisioned a tenure devoted to bricks and mortar, I felt a strong urge to plan for the building of an addition to our chapel. Ours was a growing ward, and we were overcrowded on Sunday mornings. By the end of 1977, I was convinced that we needed an addition to the building, even though our members would be responsible for thirty percent of the cost, a figure that eventually climbed to one hundred thousand dollars.

No one pressured me to do this. Although the stake president favored the idea, he had not instructed me to consider it. No members had approached me with arguments of how an enlarged building would improve the gospel program. My interests were primarily in people and counseling, and it was very much against my grain to begin a project that would be time consuming for many months. Yet I felt a spiritual impression that this building should be completed. I was moved to do it, and I became excited about it. Over several months I spent numerous hours in planning, choosing an architect, telephoning Salt Lake City, and making decisions. For one without a business background it was an enormous learning process, but I never felt like turning back. I knew that the Lord wanted it this way.

In our initial year of sacrifice, we challenged each member to donate to the building fund. For those who felt they had none to spare, we challenged them to find new ways to earn money. Marti began giving piano lessons, for instance, for our part, and that money went directly into the building fund. I began writing free-lance newspaper articles, something I had never done before, and the money went into the fund. Many ward members generated income they did not know they were capable of finding and without endangering the necessities of life. All of us felt that we had been blessed in abundance. The building process had distinctly spiritual benefits that no one could deny.

By August 1980, the new building was finished, a marvelous boon to Church activity. Our youth program grew more active and missionary work surged. The third phase helped make our ward complete in a spiritual sense, and people reacted to it positively. The worrying and fund raising were worth the effort.

These are just a few experiences suggesting that the Lord guides us in our homes, and wherever we are, and that we need to be sensitive enough to listen and respond. We may listen, but still be obstinate enough to ignore the message given, as I did at that motel in Palmyra. Clearly, the Lord does not intend to give us the answers we need for a given problem without our own solid efforts. We need to grapple with problems and make decisions of our own, but we should not hesitate to ask for the Lord's help. Successful leaders will continually seek the guidance and enrichment of the Spirit.

CONCLUSION

Leading others is one of the most challenging tasks that any of us will ever attempt. Unfortunately, almost all of us will be tempted to exercise "unrighteous dominion" over those we lead, forget the importance of human relationships, and to become carried away with the "things of this world and aspire to the honors of men." (D&C 121:34-38.) It is important to remember during those times that leaders are not chosen to be superiors over their followers, but rather, to serve their followers' needs.

In leadership, service takes many forms. At times we may have the opportunity to teach the one, while other times we may need to motivate large groups of people to realize their potential. At times we may need to express love and compassion, and at other times we may need to reprove with tact those who have made serious mistakes. At times we may need to be creative about programs and techniques, while at other times we may need to encourage people to endure to the end.

In all our desires to succeed, we should take pains to be leaders and exemplars, not managers or caretakers. We should have the courage to stand for principle, and the integrity to be what people think we are. We should be dedicated enough to tackle the job with vigor and see it through; and we should do it because of what it will mean to those we serve. As leaders we are entrusted with the worth of souls. When we're in charge, there is no greater need than for each of us to lead in humility, as we follow Jesus Christ.

NOTES

Chapter One: Leadership by Example

1. Lee, address given at stake conference in Hastings, New Zealand, April 1961.
2. Kimball, "Jesus The Perfect Leader," *Ensign,* August 1979, p. 5.
3. Bennion, *Sunstone,* February 1985, p. 17.
4. Ashton, "Unchanging Principles of Leadership," *Ensign,* June 1979, p. 58.
5. Kimball, "Boys Need Heroes Close By," *Ensign,* May 1976, p. 47.
6. Ibid.
7. Kapp, "Past 115 Years Serve as Young Women Prologue," *Church News,* December 9, 1984.
8. Kapp, "Stand Up, Lead Out," *New Era,* November 1985, p. 25.
9. Young, "By Love, Serve One Another," *Ensign,* December 1971, pp. 66-67.
10. Fyans, "How to Move the Kingdom," *Ensign,* August 1980, p. 23.
11. Brown, *Relief Society Magazine,* October 1969, p. 725.
12. Abrea, "The Sure Sound of the Trumpet," *Ensign,* May 1984, p. 70.
13. Winder, "Draw Near unto Me through Obedience," *Ensign,* November 1985, p. 96.
14. Hanks, "Practicing What We Preach," *Ensign,* June 1971, p. 90.

Chapter Two: A Lifetime of Service

1. Cannon, "Shepherds for Troubled Times," *Church News,* 1983.
2. Moss, "Sheep, Shepherds, and Sheepherders," *New Era,* June 1977, p. 21.
3. Miner and Kimball, *Camilla,* p. 175.
4. Smith, *The Love That Never Faileth,* p. 124.
5. Ulrich, "Visiting Teaching," *Exponent II,* Summer 1983, p. 15.
6. Brown, "Service," *Relief Society Magazine,* December 1969, p. 887.
7. Bennion, "Saint for All Seasons," *Sunstone,* February 1985, p. 14.
8. Kimball, "Small Acts of Service," *Ensign,* December 1974, p. 7.
9. Ibid., p. 5.
10. Kimball, *Spencer W. Kimball,* p. 334.
11. Kimball, "Small Acts of Service," p. 5.

12. Muggeridge, *Something Beautiful for God: Mother Teresa of Calcutta*, pp. 50, 68.

Chapter Three: Confidence Versus Humility

1. McConkie, "Are the General Authorities Human?" address given at Salt Lake LDS Institute of Religion, October 28, 1966, p. 1.
2. *Spencer W. Kimball*, p. 416.
3. Kimball, *Church News*, January 6, 1979.
4. Bangerter, "A Special Moment in Church History," *Ensign*, November 1977, p. 26.
5. Turley, "How Can I Have More Confidence and Feel Better About Myself?" *New Era*, November 1985, pp. 44-45.
6. Pearson, "Never Go into Winchell's without Buying a Doughnut," *New Era*, January 1986, p. 34.

Chapter Four: The Dangers of Pride

1. Packer, "The Ideal Teacher," address given to seminary and institute faculty, June 1962, p. 3.
2. *Spencer W. Kimball*, p. 412.
3. Ibid., pp. 189, 190.
4. Quinn, *J. Reuben Clark: The Church Years*, p. 37.
5. Ibid., pp., 122-23.
6. Smith, *Journal of Discourses*, 3:283.
7. Journal of Wandle Mace, p. 251.
8. Marsh, *Journal of Discourses*, 5:206.
9. Ibid., 5:208.
10. Burns, *Leadership*, pp. 448-49.

Chapter Five: Reproving with Love

1. Young, *Journal of Discourses*, 4:21, 22.
2. Diary of Thomas Bullock, September 4, 1847.
3. Pratt, *Autobiography of Parley P. Pratt*, pp. 400-401.
4. Young, *Journal of Discourses*, 1:108.
5. Taylor, *Conference Report*, April 1880, p. 78.
6. Woodruff, *Journal of Discourses*, 2:198.

Chapter Six: Reaching the Individual

1. Hanks, "Just One Boy," *Improvement Era*, December 1959, pp. 46-47.
2. Hinckley, "The Sunday School as a Missionary," *Ensign*, August 1971, p. 31.
3. Kimball, "Jesus the Perfect Leader," *Ensign*, August 1979, p. 5.
4. Dyer, "Personal Concern a Principle of Leadership," *Ensign*, August 1972, p. 70.
5. Likert, *The Human Organization*, p. 47.

6. Dyer, "Personal Concern a Principle of Leadership," p. 70.
7. Ibid., p. 71.
8. Ibid.

Chapter Seven: People Not Programs

1. Smith, comp., *Teachings of the Prophet Joseph Smith*, p. 241.
2. Kimball, "How to Try without Really Succeeding," pp. 3, 4.
3. Burns, *Leadership*, p. 297.
4. Nibley, "Leadership vs. Management," *BYU Today*, February 1984.
5. Young, *Journal of Discourses*, 13:153; 8:185.
6. Nibley, "Leadership vs. Management," p. 45.
7. Pusey, *Builders of the Kingdom: George A. Smith, John Henry Smith, George Albert Smith*, p. 255.
8. Hainsworth, "If You Would Serve Them, Love Them," *Ensign*, March 1986, p. 28.

Chapter Eight: Holding Effective Meetings

1. Naisbitt, *Journal of Discourses*, 21:44.
2. Young, *Journal of Discourses*, 12:24.
3. Ibid., 10:349.
4. Cowley, *Matthew Cowley Speaks*, pp. 386-87.
5. Ibid., pp. 398-99.
6. Kimball, "Ministering to the Needs of the Members," *Ensign*, November 1980, p. 46.
7. Funk, "Coming to Terms: A Women's Roundtable," *This People*, November 1985, p. 58.
8. Richards, *J. Golden Kimball*, p. 378.
9. Ibid., p. 353.

Chapter Nine: Teaching Correct Principles

1. Bennion, *Jesus, The Master Teacher*, p. vii.
2. As quoted by Elder Thomas S. Monson, "Only a Teacher," *Ensign*, May 1973, p. 27.
3. Hanks, "Good Teachers Matter," *Ensign*, July 1971, pp. 61-62.

Chapter Ten: The Art of Delegation

1. Burns, *Leadership*, p. 19.
2. As quoted in *Boston Globe* editorial, March 20, 1983.
3. Thomas, "A Year of Caring," *New Era*, November 1985, p. 61.
4. Dyer, "Why, How, and How Not to Delegate," *Ensign*, August 1979, pp. 14, 15.
5. Tanner, "Leading as the Savior Lead," *New Era*, June 1977, p. 6.
6. Dyer, "Why, How and How Not to Delegate," p. 15.
7. Tanner, "Leading as the Savior Lead," p. 6.

Chapter Eleven: Leading through Knowledge

1. Brown, address given at Brigham Young University, March 25, 1958.
2. Brown, *The Abundant Life*, p. 107.
3. Brown, notes of Dennis Lythgoe on Hugh B. Brown address.
4. Miner and Kimball, *Camilla*, pp. 126-27.
5. Kapp, "The Holy Scriptures: Letters from Home," *Ensign*, November 1985, pp. 93-94.
6. Rasmus, "Coming to Terms: A Women's Roundtable," *This People*, November 1985, p. 57.
7. Bledsoe, ed., *Poems by Emily Dickinson*, p. 69.
8. *Teachings of the Prophet Joseph Smith*, p. 149.

Chapter Twelve: Keeping Life in Balance

1. Warner, "Coming to Terms: A Women's Roundtable," *This People*, November 1985, p. 60.
2. Funk, "Coming to Terms: A Women's Roundtable," p. 57.
3. Winder, "Enriching and Protecting the Home," *Ensign*, March 1986, pp. 19-20.
4. Ibid., p. 21.
5. Stephan, "Reducing Stress: Welcome Thoughts for the Over-involved," *Ensign*, April 1982, pp. 22-23.
6. McKay, "Principles In Conflict," *Ensign*, January 1971, pp. 64-65.
7. Rasmus, "Coming to Terms: A Women's Roundtable," p. 61.
8. Bennion, "How and Where Is Intellect Needed?" *Dialogue*, Spring 1985, pp. 115-16.

Chapter Thirteen: When Leadership Changes Hands

1. Maxwell, "It's Service, Not Status, That Counts," *Ensign*, July 1975, p. 7.
2. Christensen, "The Successful Successor," *Ensign*, June 1975, p. 28.
3. *Matthew Cowley Speaks*, pp. 355-59.
4. Christensen, "The Successful Successor," p. 28.
5. Ibid.
6. Ibid.

Chapter Fourteen: Leading by the Spirit

1. Young, "Draw Near to Him in Prayer," *Ensign*, November 1985, p. 92.
2. Smith, *History of the Church*, 3:381.
3. McConkie, *Mormon Doctrine*, p. 579.
4. Thomas, "A Year of Caring," *New Era*, November 1985, p. 61.
5. *Millennial Star*, 68:628.

6. Dunn, address given at University of Utah Institute of Religion, November 10, 1972, p. 5.
7. Dunn, address given at Brigham Young University, March 7, 1972, p. 3.
8. Young, "Draw Near to Him in Prayer," p. 91.

BIBLIOGRAPHY

Abrea, Angel. "The Sure Sound of the Trumpet." *Ensign*, May 1984, p. 70.
Ashton, Wendell J. "Unchanging Principles of Leadership." *Ensign*, June 1979, p. 58.
Bangerter, Grant. "A Special Moment in Church History." *Ensign*, November 1977, p. 26-27.
Bennion, Francine. "How and Where Is Intellect Needed?" *Dialogue*, Spring 1985, pp. 115-16.
Bennion, Lowell L. *Jesus, The Master Teacher*. Salt Lake City, Utah: Deseret Book Company, 1980.
———. "Saint for All Seasons." *Sunstone*, February 1985, p. 14.
———. *Sunstone*, February 1985, p. 17.
Bledsoe, Robin, ed. *Poems by Emily Dickinson*. Boston: Little, Brown, 1980.
Brown, Hugh B. *The Abundant Life*. P. 107.
———. Address given at Brigham Young University, March 25, 1958.
———. *Relief Society Magazine*, October 1969, p. 725.
———. "Service." *Relief Society Magazine*, December 1969, p. 887.
Bullock, Thomas. Journal. Church archives.
Burns, James MacGregor. *Leadership*. New York: Harper and Row, 1978.
Cannon, Elaine. "Shepherds for Troubled Times." *Church News*, 1983.
Christensen, Joe J. "The Successful Successor." *Ensign*, June 1975, p. 27-29.
Coolidge, Calvin. *Cal Coolidge Autobiography*. 1929. As quoted in *Boston Globe* editorial, March 20, 1983.
Cowley, Matthew. *Matthew Cowley Speaks*. Salt Lake City, Utah: Deseret Book, 1971.
Dunn, Loren C. Address given at Brigham Young University, March 7, 1972, p. 3.
———. Address given at University of Utah Institute of Religion, November 10, 1972, p. 5.
Dyer, William G. "Why, How, and How Not to Delegate." *Ensign*, August 1979, pp. 12-15.
———. "Personal Concern a Principle of Leadership." *Ensign*, August 1972, p. 70-73.
Funk, Ruth. "Coming to Terms: A Women's Roundtable." *This People*, November 1985, p. 57-58.
Fyans, J. Thomas. "How to Move the Kingdom." *Ensign*, August 1980, p. 22-23.

Hainsworth, Susan. "If You Would Serve Them, Love Them." *Ensign,* March 1986, p. 28-31.

Hanks, Marion D. "Just One Boy. "*Improvement Era,* December 1959, pp. 44-47.

———. "Good Teachers Matter." *Ensign,* July 1971, p. 60-64.

———. "Practicing What We Preach." *Ensign,* June 1971, p. 90-92.

Hinckley, Gordon B. "The Sunday School as a Missionary." *Ensign,* August 1971, p. 29-31.

Journal of Discourses. 26 vols. London: Latter-day Saints Book Depot, 1854-1886.

Kapp, Ardeth. "The Holy Scriptures: Letter from Home." *Ensign,* November 1985, pp. 93-94.

———. "Past 115 Years Serve as Young Women Prologue," *Church News,* December 9, 1984.

———. "Stand Up, Lead Out." *New Era,* November 1985, p. 25.

Kimball, Edward and Andrew Kimball. *Spencer W. Kimball.* Salt Lake City, Utah: Bookcraft, 1977.

Kimball, Spencer W. "Boys Need Heroes Close By." *Ensign,* May 1976, p. 45-47.

———. *Church News,* January 6, 1979.

———. "Ministering to the Needs of the Members." *Ensign,* November 1980, p. 45-46.

———. "Jesus: The Perfect Leader." *Ensign,* August 1979, p. 5-7.

———. "Small Acts of Service." *Ensign,* December 1974, p. 2-7.

Kimball, Tony. "How to Try without Really Succeeding." Manuscript, November 26, 1978.

Lee, Harold B. Address given at stake conference in Hastings, New Zealand, April 1961.

Likert, Rensis. *The Human Organization.* New York: McGraw-Hill, 1967.

Mace, Wandle. Journal. Church Archives.

Maxwell, Neal A. "It's Service, Not Status, That Counts." *Ensign,* July 1975, p. 5-7.

McConkie, Bruce R. "Are the General Authorities Human?" Address given at Salt Lake LDS Institute of Religion, October 28, 1966.

———. *Mormon Doctrine.* Salt Lake City, Utah: Bookcraft, 1958.

McKay, Quinn G. "Principles In Conflict." *Ensign,* January 1971, pp. 64-65.

Millennial Star. (Liverpool, England.) 1840-present.

Miner, Caroline, and Edward Kimball. *Camilla.* Salt Lake City, Utah: Deseret Book Company, 1980.

Monson, Thomas S. "Only a Teacher." *Ensign,* May 1973, p. 27.

Moss, James R. "Sheep, Shepherds, and Sheepherders." *New Era,* June 1977, p. 20-23.

Muggeridge, Malcolm. *Something Beautiful for God: Mother Teresa of Calcutta.* Garden City, New York: Image Books, 1977.

Nibley, Hugh. "Leadership vs. Management." *BYU Today,* February 1984.

Packer, Boyd K. "The Ideal Teacher." Address given to seminary and institute faculty, June 1962.

Pearson, Carol Lynn. "Never Go into Winchell's without Buying a Doughnut." *New Era*, January 1986, p. 32-34.

Pratt, Parley P. *Autobiography of Parley P. Pratt*. Salt Lake City, Utah: Deseret Book Company, 1975.

Pusey, Merlo. *Builders of the Kingdom: George A. Smith, John Henry Smith, George Albert Smith*. Provo, Utah: BYU Press, 1981.

Quinn, D. Michael. *J. Reuben Clark: The Church Years*. Provo, Utah: BYU Press, 1983.

Rasmus, Carolyn. "Coming to Terms: A Women's Roundtable." *This People*, November 1985, p. 57.

Richards, Claude. *J. Golden Kimball*. Salt Lake City, Utah: Deseret News Press, 1934.

Smith, Barbara. *The Love That Never Faileth*. Salt Lake City, Utah: Bookcraft, 1984.

Smith, Joseph. *History of the Church of Jesus Christ of Latter-day Saints*. 7 vols. Edited by B. H. Roberts. Salt Lake City: The Church of Jesus Christ of Latter-day Saints, 1932-51.

Smith, Joseph Fielding, comp. *Teachings of the Prophet Joseph Smith*. Salt Lake City, Utah: Deseret Book Company, 1972.

Stephan, Eric. "Reducing Stress: Welcome Thoughts for the Overinvolved." *Ensign*, April 1982, pp. 22-23.

Tanner, N. Eldon. "Leading as the Savior Lead." *New Era*, June 1977, p. 4-7.

Taylor, John. *Conference Report*, April 1880, p. 78.

Thomas, Janet. "A Year of Caring." *New Era*, November 1985, p. 61.

Turley, Maurine. "How Can I Have More Confidence and Feel Better About Myself?" *New Era*, November 1985, pp. 44-45.

Ulrich, Laurel. "Visiting Teaching." *Exponent II*, Summer 1983, p. 15.

Warner, Pandy. "Coming to Terms: A Women's Roundtable." *This People*, November 1985, p. 60.

Winder, Barbara. "Draw Near unto Me through Obedience." *Ensign*, November 1985, p. 96.

―――. "Enriching and Protecting the Home." *Ensign*, March 1986, pp. 19-21.

Young, Dwan. "Draw Near to Him in Prayer." *Ensign*, November 1985, p. 92.

Young, S. Dilworth. "By Love, Serve One Another." *Ensign*, December 1971, pp. 66-67.

INDEX